LOOK UP

OTHER PRODUCTS BY
DEVARA THUNDERBEAT

ONE HEART CD
FLY HIGH CD
HAND DRUMMING BOOK
CHKARA JOURNEY CD
CHAKRA JOURNEY DVD
CHAKRA JOURNEY BOOK
CHAKRA JOURNEY POSTER
MAYAN LANDING CD
ANCIENT SUN CD
COSMIC DREAM CD
DNA ACTIVATION CD
HEMI—SYNC INDUCED CD's

ALL PRODUCTS AVAILIBLE AT
WWW.THUNDERBEAT.COM

ALL CD DOWNLOADS
http://thunderbeat.bandcamp.com/

LOOK UP

My Encounters with
ETs & Angels

Archangel Gabriel—
Picture by Devara ThunderBeat

True Story
By

DEVARA THUNDERBEAT

www.thunderbeat.com

BALBOA.PRESS
A DIVISION OF HAY HOUSE

Balboa Press books may be ordered through booksellers or by contacting:

Balboa Press
A Division of Hay House
1663 Liberty Drive
Bloomington, IN 47403
www.balboapress.com
844-682-1282

Because of the dynamic nature of the Internet, any web addresses or links contained in this book may have changed since publication and may no longer be valid. The views expressed in this work are solely those of the author and do not necessarily reflect the views of the publisher, and the publisher hereby disclaims any responsibility for them.

The author of this book does not dispense medical advice or prescribe the use of any technique as a form of treatment for physical, emotional, or medical problems without the advice of a physician, either directly or indirectly. The intent of the author is only to offer information of a general nature to help you in your quest for emotional and spiritual well-being. In the event you use any of the information in this book for yourself, which is your constitutional right, the author and the publisher assume no responsibility for your actions.

Any people depicted in stock imagery provided by Thinkstock are models, and such images are being used for illustrative purposes only. Certain stock imagery © Thinkstock.

ISBN: 978-1-4525-7719-7 (sc)
ISBN: 978-1-4525-7721-0 (hc)
ISBN: 978-1-4525-7720-3 (e)

Library of Congress Control Number: 2013911647

Print information available on the last page.

Balboa Press rev. date: 7/12/2013

I dedicate this Book to my Mother Leatrice
The one with the Pink and Golden Rays of Light*

CONTENTS

ACKNOWLEDGMENTS

I give my appreciation and gratitude to the following people for their contributions to my life and to this book.

Rosemary Near—For teaching and awakening me on my path.

Crystal and JC—For wisdom and knowledge from beyond.

Marjorie Muro—For giving me courage and acceptance.

Connie Patterson—For her full support and guidance.

Robert Archer—For his knowledge and wisdom of healing.

LionFire—For your generous help and Pow Wow drum.

Hartmut Jager—For the incredible book cover and drawings.

Jose Argüelles—For helping many people on this planet.

Sakina Blue Star—For the wonderful drawing of Salu.

John G Livingston—For his knowledge and wisdom of Life.

Celeste Korsholm—For her beautiful soul portraits.

Carolyn Holtgrewe—For my 22 DNA activation and teachings.

Dolores Cannon—For wakening the truth of my missing time.

Chief Little Summer—For being able to see through the veils.

Lisa Barnett—For her ability to read Akashic records.

Diana Rodríguez—For her support from the heart.

Nina Anderson—For the incredible hypnosis session.

Adam Yellowbird—For fulfilling prophecies.

Sheba My Dog—For being there and for protecting me.

Grand Father Martin—For his blessings to carrying on the truth. For my star family here on Earth.

AND to all my Angels, Spirit Guides, Star People, and Ascended Masters for guiding me on this Earth mission.

INTRODUCTION

I have wanted to write this book for many years, but the angels kept saying, "Not Yet."

I have been very patient and passionate about writing this story.

In January 2013, the doorway opened to reveal the truth about extraterrestrials, angels, and ascended masters.

My contact with ETs began at the age of four and continued throughout my life. It took many years for me to understand my connection with ETs and angels. All of my encounters have been positive ones, not like the negative experiences you see on television. These are false and made up by Hollywood.

This is one of the reasons why I am writing this book, to stop the fear and lies about our Star family. The ETs I have met are beautiful, loving beings and are here to help us in our awakening and ascension process.

Knowing them has confirmed my purpose and mission on this planet. The angels are closer to us than you know, and are here waiting to help at any given moment. All we have to do is ask. As Jesus said, "Ask and you shall receive."

Chapter 1

IN THE BEGINNING

My First Encounter

I was four years old when I had my first encounter with extraterrestrials.

I remember it being a beautiful, clear summer day and I was outside playing and riding my tricycle in the driveway at my home in Rochester, New York. One minute I was playing in the driveway and the next thing I remember, I was floating in midair, about 15 feet from the ground and spinning in slow motion, down towards my driveway.

I said to myself, "I am going to hit my head and that's going to hurt. I need to land on my hands." As soon as I said that, I flipped around and I landed on my hands. My cat was sitting in the driveway. When he saw me appear out of nowhere, his eyes got very big and he jumped about three feet off the ground.

Then my mother ran out of the house shouting my name and saying, "I've been looking all over for you, where have you been?"

"I've been right here playing in the driveway," I said.

"No, you haven't. I just looked in the driveway and then in the backyard. I was ready to call the police."

I always remembered that day and for years, I wondered what had really happened.

When I grew older, I began asking people what they thought it might have been. No one seemed to know. Those who were spiritual suggested that it could have been a divine encounter with God. I did not know what to think of it.

YOUNGER YEARS

My mother used to bring me to the Catholic Church because my father was Roman Catholic. She was a Native American and had to convert to being Catholicism to marry my father. One Sunday at church, when I was five years old, I remember saying to my mother, "Mom, all they want here is money"

The whole sermon was in Latin and I always looked around at the people wondering if they knew what the priest was saying. I remember having to stand up, sit down, kneel, stand up and repeat this many times through the Mass. I never knew why.

At about seven years of age, I used to look at the back of our television set and wonder why it was so thick. I even took the back off and said "it should be a lot thinner, maybe one day they will make them like that". I also found TV boring and downright stupid, however, when Star Trek first appeared that was the one TV show I liked.

When I learned about Christmas and Jesus and heard that he died on the cross, I said aloud, "Jesus, I told you it takes them a long time down here to understand things. You have to repeat the information over and over again to them." Then I would say, "What about Moses? They are forgetting about Moses." I always felt a deep connection with Moses and for some reason, I felt as though I had protected him.

When I was eight years old, I remember my Father would always draw Native American Indian chiefs while he was on the phone. One day I took a good look at the picture he was drawing and I thought to myself, we were in a past life together. You were the chief and I was your son. I don't know how I knew about past lives at that age, but I did.

When I first started the science program in elementary school, I got so excited because I thought we were going to learn about the planets and the stars. To my disappointment, we ended up dissecting a frog. We never did learn about the solar system and that is what I thought science was.

History class was also boring to me. They told stories about the cowboys, but never said anything about the Native Americans. I thought I hated history until I got out of school and learned history on my own. I then realized that I loved history when the full truth was there.

My favorite subject in school was Art. I always received straight A's in art class. I received average grades in Math until I learned Algebra. That is when I received straight A's. Algebra was quite simple to me. I found out later that Algebra is an ancient math using geometry and the field of astronomy, especially mapping the positions of the stars and planets on the celestial sphere and describing the relationship between movements of celestial bodies.

When I turned 12, I discovered astrology and I became fascinated with it. I had my personal astrology chart done, which was about ten pages long. I read that chart every six months and watched myself grow into what it said about me. I then found a book on palmistry. When I finished reading it I felt that the book was right, but there was a lot of information missing. I checked other palmistry books and felt the same way. I also taught myself how to read tarot cards.

When I was around ten years old, people used to say, when I spoke, I would speak phrases from the bible. How could that be when I never read the bible, and that everything I heard in church was in Latin?

At eleven I took piano and guitar lessons. After a year, I still could not play very well. I found that the songs and the music that I was being taught were old, corny, and boring. I quit at the age of twelve. However, I still wanted to play a musical instrument but was not sure which one.

When I was 14 years of age I was dating a man named Scott. He was a singer in a band. His drummer Ralph and I became good friends. One day Ralph asked me if I had ever played the drums before. I said that I had not, ever. He handed me his drumsticks and I sat down and started to play. I loved it instantly! It was so much fun and easy for me. While I was playing a bright light came in and filled up the room with white light. All I could see were the drums. Even they were touched by this white light. I knew at that moment that this was what I was going to be doing for the rest of my life.

Ralph said, "I thought you said you never played drums before," and I replied that I never had.

He said you sound like you have been playing for years.

The rest of the band came running into the room. "Are you ready Ralph, we heard you warming up?"

"That wasn't me, that was Devara playing the drums," he said.

"Oh, we didn't know you could play drums." I said, "It's my first time." They were very surprised because they all thought it was Ralph playing the drums.

I was so excited about playing the drums that I started taking lessons from Ralph. I asked my parents for a drum set. My father said, "Girls

DON'T play drums. Why can't you be a secretary or something else?" He was so angry.

My mother ended up buying me a drum set for my 15th birthday. I picked songs that I liked and practiced four to six hours every day and after six months, I was in my first band. I was very serious about playing the drums. I guess that is why I learned so fast. In high school, I had a chance to receive a scholarship in Art but I turned it down because I fell in love with music and eventually, I took percussion at The Eastman School of Music, a prestigious music school in Rochester, New York.

One afternoon my boyfriend's sister-in-law Pam and I were returning to her house from being at the grocery store.

As I was getting out of the car, I looked up and saw a flying saucer. It was a bright, circular light, which hovered extremely low in one place. It was so close I could see large square windows that looked like they went all the way around the ship. I said, "Wow, look at that!" I was in awe. I was not frightened at all, but Pam was. She looked up and screamed, and ran into the house. I tried to catch up to her, but she ran up the stairs and into her bedroom and slammed the door. She did not come out for three days.

When I told my boyfriend and his brother that there was a flying saucer outside and to come out with me and see it, they both said, "No, there are no such things as flying saucers. You're crazy!"

"Come and see," I said again, but they would not go outside.

The next day my boyfriend's brother came to me and said, in a threatening voice, "Do not ever mention this situation to Pam or talk to any of us about what you saw ever again." Apparently, Pam was still very frightened. The next time I saw her she would not even look at me, talk to me or come near me.

After three months of playing the drums, I invited my male friends from high school to come over to my house. I wanted to surprise them. When I started playing the drums, they began yelling at me, saying that I was into that woman's liberation thing and that is why I was playing drums. I thought they would have been proud of me. I told them I didn't even know what women's liberation was and that I loved playing drums and wanted to play in a band.

"Girls do not play drums, it's for guys only. We don't want to be your friend if you are going to play drums," they said.

I was shocked. It was definitely not, what I expected. I had to make a major decision. Keep my friends that I had known all my life or continue to play the drums, something I loved doing. Even the girls in high school mocked me. I felt so alone.

I kept practicing and teaching myself the songs I liked. I said to myself if they were my true friends, they would be proud of me. Therefore, I decided to keep playing drums and leave them behind.

I played with musicians here and there until I met a guitar player. We formed a band and played Jimi Hendrix songs and some original songs for about a year and a half.

Several years had gone by since the floating in midair incident in my driveway. I continued to wonder about it. I started asking people their opinion about what could have happened, but no one seemed to know. It was not until 2004 when I found out.

I met Dolores Cannon at a crop circle conference and I bought her book, "The Custodians: Beyond Abduction." By then I felt what had happened to me in my driveway when I was four, had been an ET encounter. As I read her book, I looked for a story like mine, but did not find one. I knew that I had to have a hypnosis session with her in order to find out what really occurred.

Dolores Cannon *is a pioneer in her practice of Quantum Healing Hypnosis Therapy and past life regressions. She is a self-published author of 17 non-fiction books composed mainly of transcripts from past life regression sessions.*

I made an appointment with Dolores in January 2004 and I finally saw what had happened. The truth was revealed.

During the session, I 'saw' myself being pulled up into a tube that appeared to be transparent. I saw a round, saucer—shaped object above me surrounded by steam *(a cloaking device that the alien ships use to disguise themselves to look like clouds)*. It had three bars of colored lights in a circle. One bar was blue, one yellow, and the other, red. I looked back towards the ground and saw my mother running out the front door of our house chasing after me. She was also pulled up inside the invisible tube.

Spaceship and the Invisible tube.
Picture by Hartmut Jager

The next thing I remember I was inside the ship and I was lying down on a silver table. I was being rolled down a hallway by a man who looked like he was made of stone.

As I passed many circular doorways, I could see inside the rooms and each room was glowing in a different color. One was light purple, one was yellow and one was light blue. They took me into one of the rooms and surrounded me in yellow, golden light. They called me 'Flying Eagle with Many Wings'. They sent me back to my driveway and I floated down until I touched the ground.

NEW YORK CITY

When I was 18, I moved a friend of mine to New York City. She was a singer and she told me that NYC was the place for me.

She introduced me to many musicians. I remember jamming with some incredible, black funk musicians who kept saying to me, "Damn girl, you're better than our drum brothers!"

One original rock band I met was looking for a drummer. After playing with them, they asked me to be in their band. Okay, but I would need to go back to Rochester and make some money so that I could move here in a month. And so I did.

I found an apartment in New York City right away. There was a psychic reader moving in downstairs at the same time I was. I did get a reading from her and she said I was going to be moving out of state at the end of the month. I said, "What? I just moved here. I'm not moving out of state." I totally dismissed what she said. I did not believe her.

The band I joined needed a singer. A couple of weeks later I saw an ad in The Village Voice newspaper: "Singer available with own recording studio." His name was Michael and he was living in Tuners Falls, Massachusetts.

We all drove out there and jammed with him. He was incredible. He said, "I'd love to record with you, would you move here? I'll give you a place to stay for free." We all said, "Yes!" We moved there at the end of the month.

Shortly after moving there, I began having déjà vu two to three times a week. It was intense. Then I remembered what the psychic said, that I would be moving out of the state at the end of the month. She had been right after all. When I return to NYC, I need to tell her.

We found out later that Michael was an ordained minister and had his own church, town, recording studio and tour bus company. They rented out their tour buses to famous bands, such as "Yes", and "Joe Cocker." It was a commune, but we did not have to join. We were there to record with Michael.

I started going to the meditations on Wednesdays and Sundays at the church and I listened to some of Michael's talks. Soon, I began to notice that my awareness was expanding to a higher vibration. After a few weeks, I realized I could hear people's thoughts. However, I didn't know I was hearing people's thoughts. I thought they were just talking aloud. It was not until I answered someone. They said, "How did you know I was thinking that?" I said, "I just heard you in your voice and I thought you were asking me a question." Then they would say, "I never said that out loud, I was only thinking it." This happened many times with different people. That is how I found out I was reading people's minds or hearing their thoughts.

We finished recording and Michael did not want to perform live, so we only stayed a few months then moved back to New York City. The first day we got back, I noticed that the people there looked depressed and dark. Although I knew that my vibration had been raised I felt very vulnerable being that way in New York City, and so I had to shut it down to protect myself.

A few days later, I looked for the psychic who told me I was going to move out of state, but she was gone. I thought it was strange for her to have moved because it was only three months ago plus no one seemed to remember her ever being there.

Eventually I got a job bartending at night in the Wall Street area. One warm summer night all our lights went out in the club so we all went outside.

Wall Street is downtown at the end of Manhattan so we all looked towards uptown. All of a sudden, we saw the lights going out in all the buildings one block at a time. It was the great NYC blackout of 1977. For weeks people talked about it being from UFOs. Both Con Edison and NYC Electric Company said it was from lightning strikes. I do not remember there being any rain at all that night. There had been talk about numerous UFO sightings days before the blackout.

The band broke up so I joined another and played around NYC for about a year. Then that band split up. I answered some ads for bands looking for drummers in The Village Voice, but all I got on the phone were the words, "A female drummer? No, I don't think so. Females don't play drums." Again the same old story.

I had to talk my way into auditions, and I did get a few of them. In NYC, whenever you audition for anything, it's called a cattle call. You stand in line with hundreds of people and you get five minutes or one song. In every audition I went to, they said I was the best out of all the drummers they auditioned. I did notice they would give me more songs to play. Many times after the audition, they would keep me waiting around while they would have a meeting with their manager or producer. However, they always ended up saying they could not take me because I was a girl and that would make it more expensive for touring. Of course, I took it personal.

I finally auditioned for a band with a female singer and she thought that it would be cool to have another female in the band. "I would have a buddy," she said. That band auditioned 70 drummers and they said that I was the best. I was only 19 at the time and the rest of the band members were seasoned musicians. We showcased for many major labels and ended up signing a contract with A&M records.

Six months later, we had a top 10 hit in Europe and we were getting ready for a tour. Right before the tour we found out the producer was stealing money from us. The band then decided to break off the contract. I was very disappointed and extremely devastated.

Jon Maye, a bass player-songwriter who lived in Rochester, New York, was calling me all the time. He wanted me to be in his band called, 'Toys', but I kept telling him that I was signed with a band on A&M Records. He said that his dream was to have a female drummer and he had heard I was top notch. When the band I was with broke up, I moved back to Rochester and joined 'Toys'. We ended up recording our first album in 1980 called Dashboard Music.

One afternoon at my parent's house in Rochester, I was standing outside with some friends. I said, "Hey, look up! There's a flying saucer." It was silver and flying very slow and low to the ground with a red light on top spinning around like a police car's light. We all watched it go over my house. Everyone saw it. One of my friends suggested that we follow it, but we never did. I never saw any UFO's in New York City. It was hard see the sky because of the tall buildings.

In 1983, the band Toys moved to Long Island where Jon was originally from. We performed in New York City and large nightclubs in Long Island. We were together for eight years.

I eventually purchased a house in Brentwood, Long Island. One night while my boyfriend and I were sitting in the living room, he said he was going to the store. As soon as he left, I saw a dark figure through my sliding glass doors that faced my backyard. It was the size of a human and was all black with black wings. Instantly, I became afraid. I ran into my bedroom and closed the door. I looked up and I saw a being in a white robe with a hood with a golden tassel belt floating over my bed. It looked like a male but I could not see a face. It was surrounded in white light. I felt a little calmer, but I did not know what to do. I crouched down in a fetal position with my head between my legs and waited until my boyfriend returned. When he got back, I ran into the living room and told him what had happened. He went outside and walked around the house but didn't see anything. The being, surrounded by white light had disappeared. I have no idea what that was all about.

One day my friend Maryann called and asked if I wanted to go to a concert at Jones Beach with her. I said, "Yes". To avoid traffic on the main highway we took the beach road from Bay Shore, Long Island to the Jones Beach Theater.

The beach road is very long and desolate for about 40 miles with no exits. There is no need for traffic lights. The only roads off the main road are small ones going to beach houses. One side of the road is the Atlantic Ocean and the other side is the bay. The road is straight and you can see for miles ahead.

On the way back after the concert, we took the beach road home again to avoid traffic. Maryann was driving and there were no other cars on the road. We had been driving for a while, when all of a sudden I saw, what looked like a traffic light, several miles ahead. I said to Maryann when did they put up a traffic light on this road? I do not remember seeing any traffic lights on the way to the concert. She said she didn't know.

I kept looking at the lights. There were three vertical lights similar to a traffic light except the color green was on top, amber in the middle, and red at the bottom. I said, "The traffic light is upside down, that is weird". When we got closer, I could see it was not a traffic light. It was three balls of light hovering over the road. When we got within ten feet from them, the three balls of light separated and went in different directions. I put my head out the window and said, "Wow, how cool! As we passed by them, they circled above us and around the car and then went towards the ocean. When I looked back at Maryann, she was so scared that she was clutching the steering wheel hard with both hands.

"Did you see that?" I asked.

"I don't want to talk about it." She kept saying that over and over again. "I don't want to talk about it."

I made a mental note of the exact area where we were. I knew some commercial fishermen who did clamming in the area. A few days later, I connected with some of them to find out if they had ever seen any colored balls of light in that area. Two out of the three-fishermen said yes, that they had seen the balls of light late at night when they were out fishing. One said, "I've been seeing them for many years. They will come around for a few days and then you won't see them for a long while.

Chapter 2

SACRED
JOURNEYS

FLORIDA

Around 1982 my mother moved to Florida and I would visit her from time to time. One year I saw an ad while I was there for a psychic fair that was at a church. I knew that I had to go. There were about twelve readers, and a woman handed me a brochure describing the entire outline of each one. I told myself that I did not need the brochure. I could just look at them and know which one I wanted.

I looked inside the room where all the readers were. I tuned into each one and narrowed it down to two readers. I found out one was the head minister of the church and the other one was a psychic teacher who could read in many different ways. I picked the teacher. I felt her energy of integrity and power. Her name was Rosemary. I found out later that she had worked as a psychic detective in Michigan on the police force for five years until she moved to Florida. She said people usually pick a certain psychic because they have many things in common. She told me a little about herself and I felt that we had a lot in common. We even shared the same astrology sign, Libra.

She asked me what kind of reading I wanted. Tarot cards, I said No; Psychometry, I asked what is that? She said, "I can take your hands in mine or a piece of your jewelry and do a reading that way." I said, "Wow, I want that kind of reading!"

The first thing she said was, "Did you know you can read crystals from birth?" She was very surprised and so was I because I did not know what crystals were.

"What are crystals?" I asked.

She said, "They are stones that store the history and knowledge of the Earth, and each one can tell you a story."

She said that I could hold them in my hand and receive the ancient knowledge of each crystal or stone, and that I knew how to do this from a past life; and that it is a form of psychometry. What wonderful news I said.

I became so fascinated with crystals that I wanted to know everything about them. While visiting Florida I ended up taking a crystal class and a psychic development course with Rosemary that enhanced my awareness tremendously. She taught how to be clairvoyant, clairsentient, clairaudient, how to do remote viewing, and about premonitions. This all comes from being open-minded, listening to your heart and asking questions from within. As Jesus said, "Ask and you shall receive."

In 1991, I moved to Florida. My mother was living there alone and getting up in her age, so I wanted to make sure she was safe and taken care of.

I met some of the local musicians while looking for a band to play with. I was thinking of a name for a band. The word Thunder kept popping into my head. Some of the names I came up with were Thunderstruck, Thunder Rhythm, ThunderBeat and Minds Eye. Little did I know what I would find out later?

After living in Florida for about six months, my whole body started to ache unbearably. It was as if I was on fire from the inside out. I was in such pain that I could not even hold a drumstick in my hand. I went to a doctor and he gave me an antibiotic. After ten days, there was no change. I went back to him again and he prescribed a different kind of antibiotic, which did not work either. When I went back to him the third time he said very sternly, "There is nothing wrong with you."

He does not know what he's talking about, I said to myself. Therefore, I went to a specialist and told him my symptoms. He said it sounded like I had multiple sclerosis. I took the test and it came back negative. Then I took a diabetes test and an HIV test. Both came back negative. Different tests went on for months. This doctor also told me there was nothing wrong with me.

I spent thousands of dollars out of my own pocket and spent six months in pain. I then thought about natural herbs, but I didn't know anything about them at that time. I sat down and prayed to God. I said, God please help me. Then I asked, "What about natural herbs?" Instantly, I heard a male voice through the top of my head saying A, B, C.

I said A, B, C? Then I began to meditate on the letter A. Immediately, the word Aniseed came to mind, then B, Burdock root, C, Comfrey. I had never heard of Burdock root or Comfrey in my life, but I heard of Anise cookies and candy.

I went to the grocery store and bought some aniseed spice, and then went to the health food store where I found the burdock root. I didn't see any comfrey, so I asked the lady behind the counter. She said they used to carry it, but the government took it off the market.

When I got home, I intuitively grounded up the aniseed in a blender. I started taking a teaspoon of aniseed and three burdock capsules three times a day. After the third day, my pain was completely gone. The herbs worked! Six months of pain, thousands of dollars later and all the doctors told me that nothing was wrong with me. I had even asked one of the doctors, "what about herbs?" The doctor said, "Oh that's a bunch of crap! They do not work. I was surprised at his reaction because I knew that some prescription medicines are derived from plants.

I then became extremely fascinated with herbs. I went out and bought a few books on herbs and I learned that burdock root was a blood cleanser and comfrey repairs damaged tissue. I could not find anything on the healing properties of aniseed. To this day, I still do not know what I had, but whatever it was, it was toxic. I was aware that Florida had many toxic gases in the soil.

It was several years later before I found any information about the healing properties of aniseed.

Aniseed

Anise is an expectorant that is also antiseptic to the mucous membranes. This means that anise does double duty: it kills germs while clearing congestion and mucus. It has the mineral content of calcium, copper, phosphorus, iron, magnesium, potassium, sodium, and zinc. The first known historical reference on aniseed was in the year 1550 BC in the famous Egyptian papyrus of Ebers. It was also used in ancient times in India, China, Greek and Roman cultures.

Since then I have been studying natural herbal remedies for years and to this day, I have naturally cured people who have had Rheumatoid Arthritis, Breast Cancer, Lymphatic Cancer, Meningitis, HIV, Staph infection and more.

When I moved to Florida, I brought my dog Sheba with me. Sheba was a very special dog to me. Before I received her, I had visions of her face and her name for over six weeks. The vision kept coming to me almost every day. They were so strong they captured me. One day I literally got into my car and drove around the neighborhood looking for her. I rolled down the window and started calling her name, "Sheba, Sheba where are you?"

I finally said I must be crazy, I know all the dogs in the neighborhood and I don't know any dog named Sheba. I told the vision to stop, and it did. I blocked it out and completely forgot about it at that time.

A few weeks later, a friend came over and asked if I would help her friends move. I said sure. We got to their apartment and walked up a long stairway. Suddenly, a dog came running down the stairs, past me and my friend and went outside. The people upstairs started yelling for the dog. 'Sheba, Sheba, get up here!" I said, "Sheba, go upstairs now" and she did. When we got up to the top of the stairs they both said, "How did you get the dog back up here?" I said, "I just told her to go upstairs and she did." They said, "That dog does not listen to anybody." "Well, she listened to me." I said. At that point, I still had forgotten about the vision and completely blocked it out.

We sat and talked to her friends for a while and then found out they were not even moving that day. The girl told us that they needed to find a home for the dog because dogs were not allowed at the place they were moving. Out of my mouth came the words, "I'll take the dog." It seemed like someone else was speaking through me. Her boyfriend then said he was going to give the dog to his friend, Joe. She said, "Joe will beat the dog," and I said, "Yeah, Joe will beat the dog, so I'll take her." I kept asking myself, why was I so adamant about having this dog? I then said, "What is the dog's name again?" They said, Sheba. I lost my breath; I looked at the dog again and remembered the strong visions I had. That is my DOG! I said to myself. Eventually, they gave me Sheba. She was six months old at the time. I had her until she was 16 years old then she died.

In 1992, I opened up a crystal shop in Florida. It was the first metaphysical shop in Sarasota.

I received my Reiki l and ll initiations from Rosemary. The word Reiki is made of two Japanese words—Rei, which means "God's Wisdom or

Higher Power" and Ki, which is "life force energy". So Reiki is actually "spiritually guided life force energy that comes through your hands. Reiki treats the whole person including body, emotions, mind and spirit. Many have reported miraculous results.

"A Reiki master transfers the ability to you to utilize this energy for healing."

On my Reiki II initiation, the room filled up with many spirits. She said one of them was a male writing down everything that was happening and telling her "don't pay attention to me just keep doing the activation." It irritated her because he was standing so close to her. I found out later it was Thoth the Atlantean/Ancient Egyptian God of wisdom, record keeper, and astrologer. He has been one of my guides for many years.

After the Reiki II initiation, we went to lunch together. We walked to a place up the street from her house. While we were walking, I saw hundreds of iridescence bubbles floating in the air next to me. I told Rosemary and she started to laugh. She said that is what happened to Japanese master Mikao Usui walking down the mountain when he received the healing powers of Reiki. Mikao Usui is the founder of Reiki healing energy.

When we arrived in the lobby of the restaurant, I grabbed Rosemary and said I think I am going to leave my body. The waitress asked me if I was all right and Rosemary said yes. As we sat down, I left my body for what seemed to be about 15 minutes. Rosemary was watching over me and said that my eyes were open, but I was gone for only a few minutes. I do not remember where I went to during that moment. She said, no worries everything is okay. We both know now that the activation was successful.

Another thing I always had a fascination for was with past lives. I believed in them greatly especially after that day when I was eight and received the information about my Father and I being in a past life together as Native American Indians. I do not know how I knew about past lives, but I knew at eight years of age. I asked Rosemary if she knew of anyone who did past life regressions. "It has to be someone I can trust," I told her. She said, "I do past life regressions." I was so excited because I trusted her immensely.

During the past life regression, I was very nervous. I had never been hypnotized or regressed before so I did not know what to expect and wondered if it would work. Rosemary explained how her sessions work. She said I would go back to a lifetime where there were still unresolved issues and any healing that needed to be done.

She started the session, and for a long time, I could not see anything. She then said, "Look down at your hands. What do you see?"

"I see a little girl's hands. I think I am five years old and I now hear children playing and laughing."

"Where are you?"

"I am upstairs locked in the attic and the children are playing downstairs."

"Are you being punished?"

"No," then I whispered, "Shhh, No one is supposed to know about me."

"Why," she asked.

"Because many people would get into trouble," I said.

"I am in an orphanage."

"What year is it?"

I looked around and saw some old dresses hanging in a closet. I said, "It's around 1770 something."

She then brought me forward to when I was older in that lifetime.

I was in a barn peeking out behind some haystacks. I was still young. I seemed to be around eight or nine years of age. A man was there and he was opening the large barn door. He told me to get back behind the haystacks because no one was supposed to see me. I got mad at him and said, "You are not my father, Ben Franklin is my Father. "Shhh get back there now!" He said. All of a sudden, the most beautiful carriage rolled into the barn. It was a cream color white with baby blue, puffed-out satin design, and decorated with strings of white pearls.

Rosemary then asked me who my mother was.

A new vision came in and it was of a woman sewing a flag. Rosemary said that is Betsy Ross. I didn't see much more after that so she brought me back.

Rosemary then asked me if I knew what my name was and I replied, yes! my name was Beth.

She then proceeded to tell me that Ben Franklin had many illegitimate children. It was common in those days because they did not have any birth control, and of course, they had to keep it a secret because of the powerful position Ben Franklin was in. She said the regression should have cleared up any issues you may have had from that lifetime now that you fully understand. Later on, I did some research on Ben Franklin. I found three of his illegitimate sons, but no mention of any illegitimate daughters.

Not too long after that, Rosemary called and said that I was one of her best psychic students. She asked me if I would like to help her on a murder case that she was trying to solve. I said yes, I would like to help. She only gave me a few details and a picture of the person who died. She did teach me psychometry where I can touch a picture or items from a person and then receive information and visions. As soon as I 'tuned in' to the picture, I got all kinds of information.

I received the story in detail of what had happened. It was like watching a movie. She wrote everything down. Rosemary told me that I was right on with a lot of the information and that they were going to check further on the new information I received. A week later she called back to tell me that the information and details I had given her, had helped the case, tremendously. She then said she could not talk more about it so we left it at that.

Yvonne, a friend of mine I met while visiting Florida said, "every time I talk, it reminds me of my friend JC." You have to meet him. She introduced me to him and his wife Crystal. He was a very spiritual man. They called him the Voice of Thunder. When I first met him, we would talk for hours about the Earth changes and many spiritual teachings. He showed me the clouds and how to read the symbols in the sky, showed me faces in the rocks, and called them rock people with the ancient knowledge. JC passed away before I moved down to Florida. I found out much later from Crystal that JC was raised by wolves. Authorities found him in the forest in Northern California. They guessed his age between twelve to fifteen years old when then found him. Crystal said, "The first thing they gave him was a candy bar" "It knocked him out for three days." The authorities thought they might have killed him but he woke up on the third day. They put him through school and then asked him if he would like to go to college. JC said yes, I would like to learn chemistry. He became an alchemist. I was totally amazed when Crystal told me that he developed the truth serum, which is now called "sodium pentothal" I asked her why would he want to develop something like that? She said JC told her "men tell lies all the time that is why he developed a truth serum so people would always tell the truth". She said after that, they kept all the files about JC a secret.

What an honor it was to have met this man.

I went to California with Crystal to visit her parents in San Jose. A few days later, we made a trip to Golden Gate Park in San Francisco. There was a large psychic fair going on. I asked Crystal if she would like to go. She said that she had never been to a psychic fair. I said we have to go you will love it!

We walked into this huge building in the park. I had never seen a fair as large as this one. The best psychics from California were there. It had sections for whatever kind of reading you wanted. There was a relationship section, a money section, and then I saw a past-life reading section. Oh, I have to go there, I said. Crystal then went to another section for her reading.

As I walked closer to the area, I saw three or four people doing past-life readings. When I saw this one woman, I knew that she was the one I wanted a reading from.

As I sat down across from her, the woman said, "All you have to do is ask me a question about a person or situation."

I asked, "Were my father and I together in a past life?" I did not tell her about the time when I was eight and thought we were both Native American in a past life, he being a chief and I, his son.

She then went into a trance. She opened her eyes half way and began speaking in a different language. I said, "I cannot understand you." She looked at me and then started speaking in English.

She said, "Yes, you were both in a past life together and you were Shawnee Indians. Your father was your son and you were a chief. Wow! I was right, but I had it backwards.

I was the chief and my father was my son.

She proceeded to tell me that my father's name was Running Deer. He was given that name because every time the tribe was teaching their traditions, he would run away into the woods. He never learned the traditions so none of the chiefs in the tribe allowed him to become a chief. He was so angry with me because I agreed with their decision not to initiate him to become a chief.

I asked her what my name was and she replied, "Chief Thunder Beat."

Instantly rivers of tears began to flow down my face. I told her that I play the drums. She said, "You are carrying your medicine over with you into this lifetime."

"Why did they call me Thunder Beat," I asked.

"Because you had the rhythm and the timing with the elements and the weather, she said. You would put your hands up to the clouds and rolling thunder would happen". I was so excited. I couldn't wait to tell Crystal.

Interesting that my father always wanted to be a chief and in this lifetime, he constantly drew Native American chiefs. He owned his own company and he made sure all his employees called him Chief. Therefore, he finally got his wish.

When we got back to Florida I began searching everywhere for information about the Shawnee Indians. I could not find anything at that time, even at the Library. I kept saying repeatedly, "I want to find out about Shawnee Indians".

One day when I was at my crystal store a woman walked in. She did a 360—degree turn and then looked at me and said, "You want to find out about Shawnee Indians, don't you?"

"Yes, yes, yes," I said. Then I told her about the past-life reading I had. She immediately said, "I know. Chief Little Summer will come to you. He is a Native American of Shawnee and Mayan decent." I was so excited!

"Is there any way I can call him?"

"No, he will come to you."

Two weeks went by and still no Chief.

The woman returned once again and asked if the Chief had shown up yet. I told her that he hadn't, but asked if I could contact him myself. She said, "No, he will come to see you."

The Chief showed up about a week later with his wife, Warm Night Rain. He came into my store and asked, "Are you ThunderBeat?" I said, "That is the name I received in a past-life reading, and they said I was Shawnee.

"That doesn't matter; you would still be Shawnee even if it was in your past. I am Shawnee too," but we need to find out for sure. There are not many of us left," he said.

"How do we do that?"

"Just stand right there."

He stood about six feet from me. Suddenly, I saw spiraling energy coming out of his forehead and entering into mine. I felt it tingle a bit, but I didn't move an inch. I just stood there. When he finished, he said, "Yes, you are ThunderBeat from the Shawnee tribe. This was 500 years ago."

He then drew me a map. He said this is your land off the Ohio River. Go there and you will recognize it. He also said I was a teacher and a traveler. The children from many tribes always knew when I was coming and were excited to see me. I was the Chief in the tribe that did the healings and maneuvered the weather for cleansing and planting. He finished by saying: "and yes, you still have this power today."

That was the time when I started using the name "ThunderBeat".

Chief Little Summer has written some incredible books. I purchased two from him—The Teachings, Volumes 1 and 2. His books were very helpful in my future UFO experiences. I am so grateful to have met him. He was so powerful and so full of wisdom.

I eventually traveled to Ohio to the area he told me. I went down to the Ohio River and as I sat there to meditate, I heard this loud machinery-sounding noise. It was so loud it echoed off the walls of the river. It was a barge carrying nuclear waste down the river. Tears started rolling down my face as my throat choked up. I felt like the Native American man in the TV commercial showing the pollution on Planet Earth.

I wondered where they were taking the nuclear waste.

I said to myself, this is terrible and it has to stop. I started coughing and feeling sick to my stomach, I prayed to Great Spirit for help in cleansing the Earth.

The next area on the map Chief Little Summer drew for me was near the Serpent Mound. The Serpent Mound in Ohio is the largest effigy mound in the world. It is 1,200 feet long and about 5 feet high. While there are several Shawnee pyramid burial mounds near and around the Serpent mound site, the Serpent site itself does not contain any human remains.

As I drove towards the entranceway of the Serpent Mound, a snake crossed my path in the road. I stopped the car to make sure he crossed safely. I was very excited because this is a high honor. In Native American culture, the symbol of the snake is transformation, cosmic consciousness, and the ability to experience anything willingly and without resistance. It is one of the ancient symbols for healing and is part of the Caduceus Medical Symbol. The wings and snake is one of the symbols for Thoth.

Ancient Caduceus Symbol

I talked to some people in the area about the Serpent Mound, They said, "No one today knows why the "Mound Builders" chose to construct a gigantic serpent, which could only be fully appreciated from the sky." They also indicated, that just recently across the way in a soybean field, a crop circle with an eye of a snake appeared, which lined up with the serpents tail. No footprints were found around the crop circle.

Serpent Mound Adams County Ohio photo by Devara ThunderBeat

ENCOUNTERS IN FLORIDA

While living in Florida on the Gulf of Mexico, the beaches were beautiful and the sand was pure white. On Sarasota Beach, people told me that the sand was made of quartz crystal. It was like walking on baby powder. Apparently, there was a huge quartz crystal reef not too far out in the water.

Sheba was part Labrador. Therefore, she loved the water. When it thundered outside, she would demand to go outside. I use to watch her running back and forth in the yard as though she was directing the thunder. She would chase it everywhere it sounded and then it would start pouring rain. I would always try to get her to come into the house but she would look at me with her beautiful big eyes and I could almost hear her say, "What, are you crazy? This is my time!"

Most dogs hide under the bed when there is thunder and lightning, but not Sheba. Now I know why I had the vision of her for six weeks before I received her. She is ThunderDog—a past-life connection, definitely.

Dogs were not allowed on the beach in my area. There was a $200 fine enforced. The closest beach that allowed dogs was a 45-minute drive from where I lived, so I had to sneak Sheba down to the beach to play in the water at 1:00 a.m. We would stay there until sunrise. The sunrises were breathtaking, with colors of pink, green and turquoise. I would always keep an eye on Sheba because the road was not too far away and she was an adventurous dog and would always run out on the road. I was always worried about her being hit by a car because the dog I had before Sheba had been killed by a car.

The third time I brought Sheba to the beach at 1:00 a.m., I was amazed at how fast the time went. It seemed like only 30 minutes had gone by and then it was sunrise. I wondered how could that be. I looked around for Sheba, but I didn't see her anywhere. I kept calling for her and I looked out to the street, but there was still no sign of her. I knew that I always kept an eye on her. How could she have disappeared? I looked all the way down the beach which was about a half of a mile there she was. I called to her and she came running towards me. She was so excited to see me more than usual. I said to myself, how could I have let her out of my sight for that long? What just happened? And It is now sunrise.

A few days went by and I heard a voice say go outside, so I did. It was 1:00 a.m. I looked up at the sky and saw a purplish—silver, almost see-through flying saucer shaped ship and a voice said, "Go to the beach, let's go for a ride." I replied, "I'm not going to the beach. Who are you?" I did not hear an answer. This happened again a few more times always at 1:00 a.m.

A few days later my mother said, "You know they are here." She was talking about the ETs. She said they have been coming inside her house. "I know mom, they have been calling me out of my house wanting me to go with them. I told them no."

I then took her for a ride to the beach and told her what happened when I took Sheba to the beach at 1 a.m. and what seemed like 30 minutes later it was sunrise. I found out later it is called missing time.

We drove to the end of the beach where Sheba was. There was an abandoned hotel there. My mother said, "That is the place where they took us the other night". I then realized that last time at the beach I must have been taken up into the ship and transported to the abandoned hotel, and that's why Sheba was in that same area. She must have followed the flying ship. My mother and I still do not know what happened in that hotel, but missing time happened to both of us several times.

STRANGE THINGS

One day, I was outside talking to a friend, when a man I did not know came over to us. Suddenly, I was giving him a message in what seemed to be, Astro Physics. I felt highly intelligent and understood exactly what I was saying. When I was finished giving him the message he thanked me and went on his way. It seemed normal to me at that moment. It did not seem strange to my friend either. I tried to remember what I told this stranger; all I could remember was that it was something to do with the molecular structure of the Earth. That happened again two more times and it was always a different person that I did not know and a completely different message.

I also experienced feeling pregnant a lot. My cycles were normal and I always practiced safe sex. I even did a couple of pregnancy tests, but they came up negative. Many years later, someone told me at a UFO conference that I might have some Hybrid children out there. I did some research on Hybrid children and here is some of the information that I found.

About Hybrid Children *www.hybridchildrencommunity.com*

The hybrid children are a genetic blend of human and extraterrestrial DNA. Now, many of the children reside in a different dimension, but they will begin arriving on Earth in the relatively near future. They are excited about coming. Everyone involved in the hybridization program, whether he or she remembers here in physical reality, made a soul agreement before coming into this lifetime to take part in the agenda to awaken humankind to our infinite expressions and reunite us with our galactic family.

After that, every time I left my house I felt that someone was following me, and when I returned I could tell that someone had been in my house. It became very disturbing.

Then I began seeing different UFO's in the daytime. One was a triangular-shaped ship, which seemed to be following me around. One afternoon, I drove over to a friend's house. When I got out of my car, I looked up and saw the triangle ship hovering very low above me. I stood there out of curiosity and watched it for a while. When I moved, it moved. It came closer to me and made no sound. I asked to know what it wanted, but there was no response.

I walked into my friend's house. I did not bother telling him because everyone always seems afraid. When I left his house, I looked up to see if it was still there but it was gone.

One of Chief Little Summer's books has a section for descriptions of crafts as he calls them. This is what he says about the triangular-shaped craft from his book "The Teachings—Volume 2."

The Triangular Shaped Craft *are survey and monitoring type of craft. These are very special because of what they monitor. The subject is you! Believe it or not, the instrumentation aboard these crafts is so delicately tuned to the thirds Density that they easily and accurately pick up on thought patterns of a person or groups of persons below. They scan or read your mind, you might say. He mentions this craft also implants thoughts into people. This information is not used to control the people of the Earth. It is useful to them to know where and how to offer their service. Their crystal-powered instruments mechanically produce the psychic of telepathy. The shape of the craft permits a broad range of undistorted data to be accumulated as it slowly moves across our skies. If the mission is considered to be routine, the craft is probably unmanned and is being remotely guided from the Mother Ship.*

Wow, after I read that, many of the pieces of the puzzle started to come together. For example, when I was giving messages to people I did not know and it explains the Astro Physics information I received.

I mentioned my UFO sightings to a few people to see if anyone else was experiencing the same thing. Most everyone said no until I met a couple John and Katharine, who told me on Indian Rocks Beach on the Gulf of Mexico near Tampa, Florida there was a place where the space ships come in. He suggested that we all go there one evening and do a peaceful connection ceremony.

A couple of weeks later we all went to Indian Rocks Beach and did the ceremony at sunset on the beach. At about 9:00 p.m., I mentioned that this looked like a flight path for planes to come in because all I can see are passenger jets going towards Tampa Airport. He said the planes stop coming in at about 11:00 p.m. Then both of them said, "Just wait and you will see."

About an hour later, he pointed and said, "There, look at the horizon over the water." We all saw a red ball of light going back and forth a lot faster than the planes do and it was not blinking. He said the red probe is making sure everything is clear for the space ships to come in. As soon as he said that, a white ball of light that looked like a star, was slowly moving in the sky from our left. It stopped almost above us and remained there the whole time we were there. Then another ball of light came in on the horizon going back and forth. This one was yellow and sure enough, a green one came in right behind it. I told them that this looked like the same three balls of light I saw on the Beach Road in Long Island NY.

The next thing we saw was what looked like a plane was coming in on the same flight path. We all watched it waiting for it to come in, but it just hovered there for about 30 minutes. We then saw another plane coming in behind the one hovering. Immediately, the first object jumped sideways. "Did you see that?" I said. They both said yes and said it must be a mother ship waiting to come in. The other plane passed over us. It was now about 11:30 p.m. and the object was still parked over the water. About midnight the object began moving slowly towards us. It finally came closer and about 10 minutes later it flew right over our heads. It was a huge, black, triangle-shaped ship bigger than the ones I saw before. It had bright, round white lights at every point with bars of colored lights on the sides. The sidelights looked like barcodes. As it passed over us, it headed towards the city. We watched it for a while and from a distance, it looked like a plane. We then saw some other small objects flying on the horizon of the Gulf of Mexico, but they never came to shore.

We packed up and went our separate ways. When I got into my car, it was 2:00 a.m. Wow, the time had gone by so fast. It was about an hour's drive home. There was no traffic on the highway so I had the road to myself. When I got off at my exit, I stopped at the red light and saw a man walking in front of my car with his head down. His energy felt spooky so I made sure my doors were locked. The light turned green and as I proceeded forward, the man turned around and jumped in front of my car. I almost hit him. I went over the median to avoid him. I could have killed him. He then ran away. I was so shaken that I had to find a police officer to tell them what had happened.

I passed by a 7-Eleven store that was open and saw a police car parked out front. As I was getting out of my car, the police were coming out of the store. I told them about the man who had jumped out in front of my car right up the street. They proceeded to the area. That was strange! I wondered what that was about. I could not sleep the rest of the night because of that man.

About a month later, I heard that a man committed suicide when he jumped out in front of a car in that same area. That had to be the same man that I encountered. If I had been the one that killed him, it would have affected me for the rest of my life. I am glad that I made the police report so the person who hit the man would hopefully, not be charged.

In 1993, the owners sold the building where my crystal shop was, so I started setting up my crystal store at Metaphysical Expos and UFO conferences.

I also got the position teaching drum lessons at the Sam Ash music store in Sarasota Florida. I was rehearsing with some musicians. They were great musicians, but seemed unorganized. It seems like everyone was going in different musical directions. At that time, we had not picked a name yet. One of the guitar players said to write down a name that I would like the band to be called. I wrote down "MINDS EYE," but said to myself, this is not the name for this band.

A few weeks later, I got a call from a bass player who was looking for a drummer. I brought my drums down to where they rehearsed. I met the guitar player and played some of their original songs. We hit it off instantly. It was Progressive Rock music and exactly the direction of music I wanted to play. I said you guys are awesome! They both said so are you! I asked. "Do you have a name for your band?" "Yes, they said, we are called "MINDS EYE". I said, "Amazing! That was the name for a band that kept coming to me." I call this 'Divine Synchronicity'.

We wrote some incredible songs together about the world situations and even some solutions to the world's problems. We played together for many years. To this day, Mind's Eye was my favorite band.

THE LOW HUM

In 1994, I saw a sign that read, "Free Hearing Test". At that time, I had not had a hearing test in many years. Being a musician, I wanted to know if I had experienced any damage to my ears from playing in rock bands for so many years.

When I went to the doctor, he said to raise my hand every time I heard a tone so I did. After about 10 minutes, he said in a surprised voice, "You can hear that?"

"Yes," I said.

He asked me again in disbelief.

"Is there a problem?" I asked.

"Well, according to your test you can hear three frequencies higher than normal and three frequencies lower than normal." He played the tones that he was talking about again and asked me one more time if I could hear the tones, and I said yes. He looked at me again in disbelief.

"You're saying people can't hear these tones?" I asked.

"Right," he said.

"Then my hearing is very good?"

"Yes" he said. "Your hearing is excellent. I have been an ear doctor for twenty-five years and I have never known anyone who could hear these frequencies."

"Thank you for telling me," I said.

This explains why I can hear a low frequency hum at night and no one else seems to. I have asked many people if they hear the hum at night and only one person I know said yes. Some said they can feel a vibration in their body, but cannot hear the hum. The hum would start in the evenings about 8:00 p.m. and hum through the whole night. Many times, it was so extremely loud that it would vibrate my body and it was hard to get deep sleep. I asked my friends if they were experiencing the same symptoms and they all said YES. It would make people feel tired and disoriented. I did some research and found out about David Ickes conspiracy theories and HAARP.

The HAARP project and its purpose are to analyze the ionosphere and investigate the potential for developing ionosphere enhancement technology for radio communications and surveillance. The signals they put out may be pulsed or continuous and at many different frequencies. David Ickes says the low frequency hum is created by HAARP.

The low frequency hum I hear is at about 79Hz.

I also checked the musical key of the hum and it was in the key of D. At that time, I had been studying the chakras for many years. The key of D is the Sacral Chakra. This is our emotional area. I do know that if the same note or tone is heard consistently for several hours, it will blow that chakra out of proportion and put your whole system out of balance. The consistent hum of the key of D disrupts everyone's emotional state. This is very disturbing.

One year when I was in Taos, New Mexico, another place where they have been talking about the hum for years, I was recording a CD with William Two Feather. During the middle of the recording session, we took a break and went outside. I instantly heard the hum and it was extremely louder than I had ever heard before. Everyone seemed to hear this one. We all talked about it. I played my keyboard to check the musical key of the hum and it was in the key of E. E is the Solar Plexus Chakra. This is where our personal power resides. As previously mentioned, hearing a consistent note for hours and days will blow out that chakra. The consistent hum of the key of E disrupts everyone's personal power and personal self-esteem. This is very disturbing.

One evening the thunder voice came in. He said, "Go to Baja California for the rising of the pyramids. Many will be gathering. You will see your star family there." They showed me a vision of a pyramid in the ocean near land.

I asked the spirit voice where in Baja? I never received an answer. Baja is huge. Psychometry is similar to dowsing. I looked at a map and dowsed Baja with my finger and felt the area the voice was talking about. I looked up the Great Pyramid on the map in Egypt and discovered that it is on the same grid line.

I spoke with Chef Little Summer and he said, "Yes ancient pyramids are rising to keep the Earth from shifting her axis. These pyramids align to the grids of the great Pyramids in Egypt. There are also ones in the northern hemisphere and many south of the Equator that are also rising. They started rising in the early 1990's."

I did not want to go alone so I asked some friends and everyone said it is very dangerous there. Therefore, I ended up not going.

In 1995, my old friend and singer, Danny was having marital problems, so I let him stay at my house for a week or two. There was a lot of drama involved.

One day after he moved out, I was burning sage in my house. This is the Native American way of clearing out negative energy. I heard a knock on the door and saw a police officer standing outside.

At that moment, I had not yet opened my doors or windows to let out the smoke. Sage smells a lot like marijuana. When I opened the door, the smoke just about covered the police officer. I said to him, this is only sage. The smoke cleared and I saw and felt his energy. He had no emotions and his energy was very stiff. It felt very reptilian. How I knew this, I do not know. He had mirrored sunglasses on so I could not see his eyes. He was looking for Danny. I told him that he moved out a few days ago, but I did not know where he was. As I was telling him this, in my 'mind's eye,' I was saying to him, pull your sunglasses down. I kept repeating this. I told him I could make a phone call to try to find out where he was. "No, that is okay" he said. Then he pulled down his sunglasses and said to me without physically speaking, "what do you think about that?" I saw the slits in his eyes. I was right. He was a reptilian. I answered without physically speaking as well, "Okay, I just wanted to know." Then aloud I said, "Have a nice day officer." He went on his way. I never saw him ever again.

The next Metaphysical Conference where I set up my crystal booth was in Tampa, Florida. I met a woman there named Delfina Rose, who was speaking at the conference. Part of her story was when she was young she had been struck by a lightning bolt out of a clear blue sky. She died instantly, but after five minutes, she came back to life. As she was coming back from her near death experience, she saw hundreds of symbols that she calls star symbols. She has written a book called "Star Song Oracle: The Original Lemurian Divination Amulets" that includes star cards. She said after that experience, she could put her hand through any physical object.

She was also giving psychic readings at the conference. She was so amazing that I had to get a reading from her. I scheduled a time, and at the reading, I asked her a question. She said, "Wait. First, I have to tell you something very important. She startled me. I said Okay.

Did you know you were a Mayan High Priestess not too long ago?"

"No" I said

"What's not too long ago?" I asked.

"A thousand years ago. Do you know about the Mayans?"

"I know a little bit about them," I said.

This is very important for you to know because you have some work to do with the Mayans in this lifetime.

She also said that I was from the future and that I had made an agreement with the Star people to help the Earth people with the upcoming shifts. At that time, I did not know what she meant. This was in 1995.

Now I was very curious about the Mayans and being a Mayan High Priestess. I always had an attraction and a calling to go to Belize. I was fascinated about what she said so I started to do some research on the ancient Mayan culture and I discovered there was little information available at that time.

The rest of that year, I was performing with Mind's Eye and was teaching at the music center.

1996

At the next Metaphysical Conference, I brought my friend Crystal with me. I remember sitting at my booth when Crystal handed me a picture of a wall painting with hieroglyphs from Egypt. I was trying to decipher it when all of a sudden I heard a male spirit's voice telling me to turn around. I turned around and there was a woman with brochures in her hand saying "Trip to Egypt 11:11:11 ceremony in The Great Pyramid". I looked back at the Egyptian picture in my hand and said, Okay, Great Spirit I understand. I will go and talk to the woman with the trip to Egypt.

She said her name was Carol and her company was called Sun Da RA Tours. She gave me the details about the journey and the price was $3333. I did not have the money at that time, but I knew that I was supposed to go on this journey. When I got home from the conference, I sent her half of the money for the trip. I had about three months to come up with the rest.

At the end November in 1996, just before I went to Egypt, My friend Rena invited Crystal and I to a five day Star Knowledge Conference in Estes Park, Colorado. She had some free passes. It represented the beginning of the Mayan 15-year cycle of transition from Fourth to Fifth World. We stayed on the premises in the park. One day while I was there, I went down to the small town. I was in one of the shops when I saw this postcard. It was a rock formation called "Twin Owls." I immediately knew I had to go to this place. She said, "Oh, it's just right around the corner." I jumped into the car with Rena and said we have to go to this place now! It is calling me.

We went through the entranceway and drove past some large square rocks. I immediately felt and said, "This is Mayan and those square rocks we just passed is a doorway.

Rena said she did not feel like it was Mayan. "I feel it very strongly," I said.

We drove around and saw The Twin Owls rock formation. I kept feeling there was something else I was supposed to see. I drove Rena back to the retreat and then told Crystal that I had to take her to this amazing place.

Crystal was a rock hound and she played crystal bowls so beautifully. I wanted to see what she felt. I did not tell her that I felt it was Mayan. I drove her through the doorway of rocks and she immediately said, "This is Mayan!" I said, "Yes, I feel the same way."

I told her there was something we were supposed to see and Great Spirit says it is very large. We drove around for about 10 minutes, and sure enough, Crystal found it. It was an ancient Mayan High Priestess' face in the rocks.

Mayan High Priestess Estes Park Colorado—
photo by Devara ThunderBeat

Wow, I knew I felt Mayan energy here. Maybe this is where some of the Mayan ended up during the Spanish invasion in Mexico. One day I want to go to the Mayan lands. Remembering what Delfina Rose told me that I was a Mayan High Priestess 1000 years ago. I need to go there to see if I recognize anything.

Journey to Egypt

Egypt Pyramids—Photo by Mohammad Alibe

When I returned home from the Star Knowledge Conference, I had only a few weeks before leaving for Egypt. All of a sudden, the rest of the money I owed for the trip dropped into my lap, so to speak and extra for things I wanted to buy while I was there. It seemed like it came out of nowhere. Woo, woo!!! I knew I was supposed to go. It was Divine synchronicity. The group was leaving at the beginning of January 1997. Carol mailed us the itinerary and a list of what to bring.

The week before my journey to Egypt, I received a strong message from Spirit. A loud thunder voice came in and said, "Activate the generators below The Great Pyramid with your drum. They have been dormant for a while. They need to be activated to help the Earth stay balanced on her axis." "Okay, I am on the mission," I said. I do believe this was another Divine mission I was asked to do.

Then before I left, every day I kept hearing in my head the theme song from the movie Love Story. I did not know what that meant until later.

On January 7th 1997 I left for Egypt. The group was meeting at JFK Airport in New York. I did not know anyone in the group except for Carol, the coordinator. I remember reading in the itinerary about the spiritual guide who was going to be with us. I was excited to meet her.

When I got to JFK airport our plane was delayed a day so we were put up in a hotel. We all had dinner together and I got the chance to meet the spiritual guide. I said, "Hi my name is ThunderBeat", and I touched her on her shoulder. She just glared at me with dark piercing eyes and said, "Don't ever touch me!" Ouch, this was going to be interesting, I thought.

There were about 26 of us in the group. The rooms were based on double occupancy so I was assigned a roommate. My roommate was Toni. She was so sweet.

It was a 16-hour flight and we got into Egypt late afternoon. At dinnertime, I was able to talk to more of the people in the group and instantly made some wonderful friends. I met Everett and his wife at dinner. We could see The Great Pyramid from where we were staying.

We were all so excited to see the pyramids. Everett said, "The tour does not start until tomorrow at 10:00 a.m. I am going out real early in the morning to the pyramids. I met a person who has camels and horses that will take us there. Come with us." I said, Okay!

We were all to meet in the Lobby the next morning. I was so excited I couldn't sleep. It was 6:00 a.m. when we got to the stables. I picked a horse and my roommate Toni came with us and picked a camel.

It appeared that the stable people were stalling. Everett said, "C'mon let's go!" The owner told his two young sons to guide us out to the desert. When we got there, the pyramids were still pretty far away. Wow, they were huge. I took some pictures. There were no clouds in the sky except for one cloud formation right above the middle pyramid. I looked at it through my camera zoom lens, and the figure looked like Isis. She appeared to be wearing a long cape with her hands stretched out, and she had a throne on her head, the symbol for Isis. Incredible, how magical this is. The Ancient ones are still here.

Isis is an ancient Egyptian goddess who represented magic, motherhood, healing, resurrection, prophecy and the arts she taught her people many skills in agriculture and they worshipped her as the goddess of medicine and wisdom. They say Isis and her husband Osiris were from the planet Sirius.

The sphinx was the closest to us. Everett told our guides to go to the sphinx, but they shook their heads no. We then continued riding along the edge of the area. Everett said, let's go this way and we all followed him towards the Sphinx. All of a sudden, the police came out of nowhere. The two sons jumped off their horses, left us there and ran away.

I said, "What is going on?"

The police said, "You are all under arrest". You are not allowed to be here at this time. This area does not open until 9:00 a.m.

I thought, oh no we are all going to jail and it is our first day in Egypt.

Everett pulled the officers aside. Then all of a sudden the police officers said, "Go back with the camels and horses, now!"

I found out later Everett gave the officers some money to let us go. Whew! Thank God for that!

That day we proceeded on our journey as originally scheduled. We headed out to Saqqara located south of Cairo. This is where one of the oldest complete stone buildings called The Pyramid of Djoser or Step Pyramid is.

There are many ancient underground tombs in that area. We went down into one of the tombs that they have found for King Onas 2475 BC. It had many rooms. With my third eye, I could see the different colors of each room. Colors are frequencies that have and hold special knowledge. The colors looked to be the same as those of the ship I was on when I was four years old.

One room I was very fascinated with had Ancient Egyptian writing on all four walls and stars on the ceiling. They were not the regular hieroglyphs that you see in the other temples. I sat in there and meditated until they said we had to leave. They said it was a tomb but it did not feel like that to me. It was more like a library, or a school with universal knowledge.

King Onas Tomb—Photo by Devara ThunderBeat

We had an Egyptologist tour guide and everyone was to follow him. I listened to him for a while, but felt there was a lot of missing knowledge and misinformation. I needed to connect with the energies of the temples by myself.

While walking alone in Saqqara I found some round circles of white crystal stone embedded in the ground. They were about a foot and a half in diameter and they sparkled and glittered in the sun. I reached down to touch them and a few pieces of stone came off in my hand. I stood up and looked at them. Then all of a sudden, I looked down and saw a scarab crossing my trail and the crystal stones in my hand started to vibrate. The stones flew out of my hands and I looked back down at the scarab and it was gone. I picked up the stones again, and at that time, they were not vibrating... HMMM?

After that, we went to a newly uncovered site that was not on the itinerary. We were told it was a Hathor site. The Egyptologist said not to touch anything because nothing had been recorded yet. We went down into the archaeological site and the spiritual guide asked us to make a circle for a ceremony. I was standing next to Everett and his wife.

According to Tom Kenyon's channeling of the Hathors, the Hathors say that they are a group of interdimensional, intergalactic beings who were connected to ancient Egypt through the many Temples of the Goddess Hathor. They use sound to heal.

Hathor Photo by Mohammad Alibe

A few minutes later, I felt a dagger-like energy on my back. I turned around and looked up and saw a man standing on the high ledge looking down at us. He was wearing a full black suit with gloves on and dark sunglasses. I said to myself, it is excessively hot to be wearing a suit. I turned back and said to Everett "there is a man in black behind us watching what we are doing. He turned around and said, "You're right. Don't look at him."

This man's energy was intense. It felt robotic and very authoritative, commanding and threatening not to touch anything. I turned around a few minutes later and he was gone.

Before I went to Egypt, I was hearing a lot about Men in Black. His energy was exactly what people had been describing. At that time, the movie "Men in Black" was not out yet. The movie was nothing like what I had experienced. Here is some information on Men in Black.

Men in Black *From Wikipedia: in American popular culture and in UFO conspiracy theories, are men dressed in black suits who claim to be government agents who harass or threaten UFO witnesses to keep them quiet about what they have seen. It is sometimes implied that they may be aliens themselves. The term is also frequently used to describe mysterious men working for unknown organizations, as well as various branches of government allegedly designed to protect secrets or perform other strange activities.*

I told a friend of mine Arcturus Ra, the men in black story and he said that since the site had not been searched there are activation tools there they do not want anyone to know about.

We are scheduled to go to the Great Pyramid overnight in a few days. I was excited about activating the generators in the Great Pyramid. I found out you can make a reservation months ahead of time for an overnight stay, but at a hefty price.

At lunchtime, I met two powerful women, Marilyn and Linni. Marilyn was talking about doing ceremony in the temples. She brought her crystal bowls and Linni brought tuning forks. I told them that I would be buying a drum in Egypt as soon as possible. Marilyn mentioned that she did not like the spiritual guide and did not want to do ceremony with her. We all agreed to do ceremony together.

After the tour that day, I went down to the local shopping area in Giza to buy a drum. I planned to buy one for the activation in the Great Pyramid and for some ceremonies.

I definitely wanted an Egyptian Doumbek Drum, wood, if possible. Most Egyptian drums are made of ceramic and aluminum. I walked into a shop that made mosaic tile. The first thing I saw was a hand drum inlayed with mother pearl. Wow, that is beautiful. That has to be expensive, I thought.

I asked the man in the store if he made the drum. He said yes that he had put the inlay on and just finished it a couple of days ago. Each intricate piece of mother pearl had been cut by hand, in the Sedef inlay technique, (Sedef is the Turkish name of mother of pearl) the craftsman glues them in their spot then waits for a couple of days to dry before sandpapering and waxing. Usually, floral designs are used. These drums cost $400.00 or more. I played it and it sounded very nice. This one was made of wood and was lightweight. Ceramic drums are heavy to carry around and I had a lot of traveling to do. I asked, "How much for the drum?" He said $60.00. What an incredibly low price, I thought. "I'll take it!" "What a beautiful drum I have to do ceremonies with. I feel blessed. Thank you God!"

The next day the spiritual guide did not show up.

Linni told me that Marilyn summoned for the group, "Whoever does not tell the truth will be silenced." After that, we did not see the spiritual guide for three days.

A few days later, we flew to Aswan, which is about the middle of Egypt on the Nile. There was also a side trip to Abu Simbal that day, which I took.

Abu Simbal is located at the southern tip of Egypt. Therefore, we had to take another flight from Aswan. Half the group went. We boarded the plane, and as soon as it took off and in the air, we heard a loud explosion. We were all waiting for the pilot to say something, but he never did.

I was sitting next to one elderly man from the group. He said it sounded like we blew out a tire. He said that he used to be in the air force and he was sure that is what it was. The spiritual guide was on the plane with us and she was crying and saying, "Oh, no, we're all going to die!"

I tuned into my spirit guides, and heard everything will be all right. The Egyptologist went and talked to the pilot; he came back and said we will be making an emergency landing at the military airport. When I asked him what was wrong he said that the pilot does not know.

As we were beginning to descend, I looked out the window and saw the airport. There were fire trucks racing on the runway towards us. I said to the man next to me "do you think that is for us?" He said, "Probably so."

It was the smoothest landing I have ever experienced. We all had to get off the plane. We landed a long distance from the building where we had to walk too. When I got off the plane I looked back and saw a shredded tire, I wondered how we made such a smooth landing. I looked around at the terrain and felt a strong presence of ET energy. Hmmm We all had to go into the main building and we were strictly told not to go outside. There were guards with rifles at each door. After waiting around for about thirty minutes, I was curious about the ET energy I felt. I went to the back door where I felt the presence and started talking to the guard. While I was talking to him, I was looking around. I was looking at the many sand dunes, when all of a sudden I saw a circular silver space ship come up over one of the dunes very low to the ground and fly quickly by. Right away, I knew it was a worker ship. How I knew that, I don't know. The guard was not sure if I saw the space ship, but he told me to go back inside the building NOW and stay inside.

The craft was saucer-shaped and the color was silver-chrome. It was very shiny and it reflected the sand underneath the bottom of the ship. Now, I know the Egyptian's are working with ETs.

Picture by Hartmut Jager

We finally boarded the same plane and headed out to Abu Simbel. Some of the people in the group were still nervous. I was excited about seeing Abu Simbel. As we were flying, I was looking out the window at the terrain and saw more pyramids. The Egyptologist said there are no pyramids in that area. He asked, "What are you looking at?" and I showed him.

"Those are not pyramids. They are rocks that look like pyramids."

It seemed to me that he was covering up something. So far, they have found 70 pyramids in Egypt. Many years later, some pyramids were discovered in that area.

ABU SIMBEL TEMPLES

The Abu Simbel temples are two massive rock temples in Abu Simbel in Nubia, southern Egypt. They are situated on the western bank of Lake Nasser. The twin temples were originally carved out of the mountainside during the reign of Pharaoh Ramesses II in the 13th century BCE, as a lasting monument to himself, the gods and his queen Nefertari, to commemorate his alleged victory at the Battle of Kadesh, and to intimidate his Nubian neighbors. However, the complex was relocated in its entirety in 1968, on an artificial mountain made from a domed structure, high above the Aswan High Dam reservoir.

The relocation of the temples was necessary to avoid their being submerged during the creation of Lake Nasser, the massive artificial water reservoir was formed after the building of the Aswan High Dam on the Nile River.

Abu Simbel—Egypt Photo by Mohammad Alibe

We were about an hour late so we did not have much time to see this remarkable site. I was awestruck. I walked inside the Ramses II Temple and I was energetically pulled straight back to a chamber. I looked inside and saw four large figures sitting side by side on their thrones. I immediately kneeled down to honor them and then messages started coming through. They told me that this is the meeting place of the Gods. I heard each one of them in their own voice telling me their purpose. Honor, Will, Knowledge, and Soul. I thanked them for the information and since we did not have much time left, I quickly walked over to the Nefertari temple. This is on the far right of Ramses temple.

When I walked back to Ramses temple the group said, "Come on you're late, we need to catch our bus."

I still wanted to see some things so I told them I would be right there. As I was admiring the outside of Ramses II Temple, all of a sudden the temple guard came up to me and said "you have to go." You are late for your bus here, take this short cut. He then proceeded to take me to the right side of Ramses temple. He opened up a huge stone door and said "Go inside and follow the wooden pathway to the end and you will see a doorway." He closed the door behind me. I then realized I was inside a hollowed-out mountain. It was all lit up inside and there again I felt ET energy.

While walking up the wooden planks I had a feeling that I was being watched, like a whole group of beings observing every move I made. I felt like I had entered into another world. It became very dark at the top of the wooden planks as I was holding on to a flimsy guardrail. I finally got to the top and opened up the door. The sun was extremely bright but I could see the bus. When I got on the bus, I asked a few people in the group if they went inside the mountain. Everyone said, "What are you talking about?" I told them what had happened and the Egyptologist said there is no doorway inside the mountain that would take you to the top where the bus is. Hmmm??

That evening we boarded our cruise ship. We would be sailing on the Nile for the next four days.

The next day we went to the Isis Temple. It was a beautiful clear day with not a cloud in the sky. Marilyn and Linni suggested that we do a ceremony at the Isis Temple together and invite those who wanted to join us. Almost everyone did.

Marilyn, Linni and I set our intentions, performed an initiation for the group, and did several affirmations. I did a heart into the light ceremony that releases fear and brings more love into your life. After the ceremony, I looked up and saw a rainbow in the sky. There were no clouds. It was not a sundog and not everyone could see it. I have never seen a rainbow in the sky without the presence of rain before. It was beautiful and to me, a sign of work well done.

After that, we did a ceremony with the spiritual guide. I did not understand her intentions because her ceremony had nothing to do with Egypt or why we were there.

We returned to the cruise ship and sailed to the Temple of Kom Ombo.

The spiritual guide told us that Kom Ombo was an extremely powerful place and that we are going to do a special sacred ceremony there. She was very excited about this temple. I made sure that I had my drum with me. The layout of the building combines two temples in one with each side having its own gateways and chapels.

Kom Ombo is a double temple, dedicated to Sobek the crocodile god (above left), and Horus the falcon-headed god (above right). Photo by Mohammad Alibe

It was early evening when we got there and the temple was lit up. In the front courtyard by the entranceway, there was a high tower. I looked up and felt the energy. I said aloud, "this was a prison." Linni and Marilyn heard what I said.

The Egyptologist said we could go everywhere in the temple. Then he pointed to the left and said, but no one is allowed to pass through that doorway. I looked at the area he was pointing to and saw that it was blocked.

While we walked around, I saw several Roman statues with their heads cut off. Obviously, there was a lot of violence here. The spiritual guide then gathered us all together and said we needed to do a ceremony now because it is a long procedure and it is getting dark.

She explained it was the crocodile ceremony. She heard about this ceremony from one of Drunvalo's books. She showed us a pit and two doorways where they used to keep the crocodiles. There was a maze underneath that no one could see. She said that each person would go through the maze alone. The temple was lit up, but since there was no light down below, you will not be able to see where you are going and will have to crawl because it is only three feet high. I said, "If no one can see then we need to have a drum playing at each doorway so they can hear their way through". She agreed.

There was another person in the group with a drum. I had him sit at the exit of the maze and play a steady rhythm. I sat at the entranceway and played the rhythms for the group so they would know the differences and then they would know where to go. The rhythm that came through me I found out later was an ancient Egyptian ritual rhythm. The drumming was very relaxing and meditative.

None of us knew what to expect or how long it would take for each person to go through the underground maze. The first person to come through said "Wow! You cannot see a thing and it's a labyrinth." It took this person approximately seven minutes to go through the maze.

It was now getting down to the last person. A person from the group said it was my turn. I handed my drum to the person next to me and had him play the rhythm; it was hard for him to play so I showed him an easier version. I knew I needed the sound of the drum to go through this maze.

I proceeded down the large blocks of stone. I then had to get on my hands and knees. All I kept thinking was there used to be water with crocodiles down here. As I moved through the maze, it became completely dark. I could hear both drums. I said to myself, I want to be able to see so I can go through this quickly. Then suddenly, I could see. There was a dim glow of light. It was like looking through night vision goggles. Then I noticed I could feel with my body exactly where the walls were. I became very agile and was able to maneuver rapidly. I slithered through the maze like a snake. I came up to the exit and had to climb up some large stones. At that point, it became very difficult for me to move up the stones. Everybody at the exit said, "How did you get through so fast?" I tried to speak, but couldn't. They asked me again, how did you get through there so quickly? I finally got to the top of the stones and said, "All I know is that I think I shaped-shifted into a snake." I had never experienced anything like that before. I don't know how that happened; all I remember was that I asked if I could see in the dark and get through this maze quickly. They told me that I went through the maze in half the time of everyone else. It only took me a few minutes. It was amazing how I could feel where the walls were without touching them. Now I know how animals can maneuver in the dark.

We all completed the ceremony and had a little more time to walk around. I kept hearing voices coming from the area where we were not allowed. As I got closer, I heard someone calling for help. "Help us, help me. Help us. Please, help us get out of here."

I walked into the forbidden area. I saw a thick, stone arched doorway with bars and an old man with long, gray hair and a long gray beard holding onto the bars. He was a spirit trapped in an ancient prison. I could see a deep tunnel behind him. With my third eye, I looked all the way down to see if there were more people. Yes, there were women, children and men trapped deep, down below. I knew that this was a prison. My feelings were right.

I immediately began playing my drum, and the most erratic sounds and rhythms came through. I kept repeating to all the spirits trapped, "Go towards the light. Go towards the light." Marilyn and Linni came running over and asked me what was wrong. I said there are hundreds of spirits trapped in that doorway with the bars. They both looked over at the prison and did not see the old man spirit, but they believed me. They both walked next to the bars and started chanting with me.

"Go towards the light. Go towards the light!" Then all of a sudden, I saw a spiral of spirits coming out of the prison and going up towards the sky. The two girls still could not see what I saw. I thanked them for helping me. I told them again that this had once been a prison and that many spirits had been trapped since the ancient times. I could tell because of the clothes they were wearing.

After that, it was time to leave. The Egyptologist said you know you were not supposed to be in that area. I said we had to remove some trapped spirits. He had never worked with a spiritual group before, and he looked at me with a puzzled look.

On the way out, there was a market. There were some men standing around who were selling drums. I picked one up and started playing. The men at the market looked stunned. They said, "You're a girl, how did you learn to play drums like that?" I just laughed and I pointed to the other drums for them to play with me. We all ended up playing drums together, laughing and having a lot of fun. I bought a drum from them. This is the type of drum Egyptians use for belly dancing and celebrations.

That evening on the cruise ship, Marilyn, Linni and I talked to the Egyptologist. We asked him about the information he was telling the group. He explained that all Egyptologists have to go through four years of college and they are not allowed to speak about certain ancient information. If they do, they could lose their authorization to be an Egyptologist. However, he did admit that some of the hieroglyphs meanings he describes were not true, but he also gave us some of the true meanings. There is knowledge they do not want anyone to know. It is ancient, sacred and powerful.

I knew it!

The next day we sailed to Edfu where a bus was waiting to take us to the Horus Temple. The temple was powerful. There were several rooms with many stories that were written in hieroglyphs. I heard they were stories of creation and the building of the Horus temple and the story of Horus and Seth. Again, I felt it was a school and a healing chamber. I heard a musical tone throughout the temple. It was the key of A, which is the third-eye chakra. Yes, that made sense, the Eye of Horus.

After walking around Horus temple for a while, I kept hearing a big, thundering voice saying, "Get out of my temple. Go Now!" It must have been Horus speaking.

I left the tour early in honor of the voice. I was the first one on the bus. Usually I am the last.

Horus Temple—Photo by Devara ThunderBeat

When I was there again in 2008, I heard the same voice saying the same thing. Horus was speaking. The energies of the Ancient ones are still there.

The next day we took a ferryboat across the Nile to Thebes to the Valley of the Queens and the Valley of the Kings. Inside the Queens tombs, there were spectacular paintings in full color of the Queens, the Gods and Goddesses. The paintings covered the walls, and stars covered the ceilings.

The Queens' tombs are smaller but more elaborate than the Kings tombs. The Queens were highly praised.

I was drawn to a blue being that was painted on the wall. I started to cry and I don't know why. I have seen the blue ones on walls at the other temples but this one looked and felt familiar, I did not want to leave. Linni had to come and get me. She said it was time to leave and we had to go now. I found out later the blue beings are the cosmic ones.

The next stop was Queen Hatshepsut's temple at Deir el-Bahari. I never saw any pictures of this temple before I got there, but I totally recognized it. The left side of the temple was in shambles. I kept saying there was a courtyard to the left down below where they used to teach the children. The living quarters were above the stairway.

Queen Hatshepsut presumed the throne as a pharaoh and wore a beard and male ceremonial clothing. She claimed legitimacy through a divine birth. Queen Hatshepsut renovated the coronation hall statuary depicting her father, Tut Moses I, her highly regarded predecessor, as a god. In the center of the hall, she installed two, 10-story red granite obelisks and a beautiful red quartz chapel.

Hatshepsut Temple Photo by Mohammad Alibe

Ten years later, I find out during an Akashic Records past-life reading why I recognized Hatshepsut's temple. The reader's name was Lisa Barnett. I asked her about my Egyptian past lives and she said I had six lifetimes there. She talked about one of my significant times. She said my name was NeferRaRe and I was the sister of a queen. She said I taught the children in the courtyard with Master Thoth and one of the children was Moses. I asked her who the Queen was but she did not know. I researched the name NeferRaRe, but did not come up with any information at that time.

Eight months after the reading, on the Discovery Channel, a program about Egypt was on. Dr. Zahi Hawass was looking for Queen Hatshepsut's mummy. They found the family tomb near the temple at Deir el-Bahari. When he opened up one of the caskets, he said, "Okay, we found a female and her name is NeferRaRe. It says she is the sister of Queen Hatshepsut." I almost fell off my chair. I just sat there and stared at the mummy saying "Wow! That is me over 3500 years ago."

In ancient Egypt, no one has the same name. They do not repeat names as we do in the United States or other countries. It was impossible for Lisa, the past-life reader to know my name because it was not discovered yet when she did the reading.

Now, more of the pieces of who I am have come together. Like Chief, Little Summer said, "the past is part of who you are." That is why I recognized Hatshepsut Temple. Now I know why I had this heart connection with Moses, I taught and protected him. Tut Moses I was my father and Queen Hatshepsut was my sister, and Deir el-Bahari is where I lived.

Our next stop was Karnak. In ancient times, this temple was open only to the priests and the pharaohs. The common people could only enter the first courtyard where they received messages and healings from the pharaoh and the priests.

The night before Marilyn, Linni and I talked about doing a ceremony at Karnack. I prepared a ceremony called the ritual of the Shent bird. It is an Egyptian heron bird with similar properties to the Phoenix bird, meaning transformation from the ashes into the light.

The next morning we told the group on the bus to Karnack that we would be doing a ceremony and all were invited. We found a nice altar at Karnak to do the ceremony.

Many from the group came. The spiritual guide did not show up. Marilyn said for me to go first.

I started the ceremony. In the middle of the ritual, many of the women were crying. It was a very positive ritual so I wondered why they were crying. As soon as I finished, Marilyn started playing her crystal bowl.

All of a sudden, I heard a Thunder voice telling me to go and sit on top of the ledge next to the ceremony. I thought to myself, I do not want to break the circle, but then the voice came in again. "Go now and sit on top of the ledge."

I noticed the high ledge to the right of where we were. I looked at one of the women in the group and moved out of the circle. She took my place. I was greatly relieved.

I climbed up onto the ledge, which was about 10 feet high. I was looking over the ceremony. The ledge was about 12 inches wide to sit on and behind me was a 30-foot drop. I didn't know why I was there. I put my hands out towards the ceremony to send them energy. Suddenly, I felt this heavy weight on my shoulder blades. It pulled me back, and I thought, "Oh no!" I am going to fall down the 30-foot drop. When I looked back, I saw seven foot long wings on each side of me. They had different shades of whites and grays. I caught my balance and then the thunder voice came in again. He said, "Go down to the courtyard." The group was still in ceremony, so I climbed down and walked into a large courtyard.

No one was in the courtyard. I thought that was strange because there were a lot of buses outside and people everywhere. I was standing in the middle of the courtyard looking around when all of a sudden I heard layers of female voices singing above me to my left and to my right.

I listened to the song they were singing and it sounded familiar. Then the singing stopped. Immediately in front of me a pharaoh appeared. I could feel his powerful energy even though he looked small. He had a headdress on of a king of Lower Egypt. He looked at me and spoke the words, "in the court of the Crimson King." The female voices came back and began singing again. In the excitement, I did a 360° turn. When I turned back, the figure and voices were gone but I felt the energy of incredible bliss.

I went looking for the group to tell them what had happened, but I could not find them anywhere. I went back to the bus, no one was there either. I didn't know how long I was in the courtyard or how much longer we had at Karnak. I sat down and rested. Wooo! What an incredible experience.

I went back towards the obelisks at the front of the temple and touched them to see if I could feel what their purpose was. I knocked on them and I heard ringing sounds. Then I saw the group coming.

"Everett, I said, Check this out! Put your ear on the obelisk. I knocked on it and heard it ringing. Did you hear it ringing?"

Everett said, "Yes, that's wild! I said these are antennae's to the stars.

When I was in Egypt, eleven years later in 2008 at Karnak, I knocked on the obelisk and they did not ring. All I heard was a solid knock on the stone. Hmmm?

I did not mention my experience to Marilyn and Linni about seeing my wings and the pharaoh in the courtyard until later that evening. When I told them the story they said, "Oh! We wondered why you left the circle." Marilyn said the female voices you heard were the Hathors singing. They both said; "What a Divine experience."

Then later that evening at dinner, I asked the people why they were crying at the ceremony. To me, it was uplifting. I read again, what I spoke and all of them said, "I heard something totally different." We talked about it for a while and everyone took turns saying what he or she heard. Each heard something completely different. Everyone received his or her own personal message. It was Divine guidance for everyone. What a magical place Karnack is.

After dinner, we went to the Temple of Luxor. Again, I felt it was a school, and this one was for all ages.

The following morning I remembered the song I heard at Karnak and wondered why it sounded so familiar. I said "in the court of the crimson king." That's it! There was a band from the 70's called King Crimson and they had a song called "in the court of the crimson king." I had a copy of their album at home. When I got back home I played it, and sure enough it was the same song I had heard at Karnak but it had all male voices on the album whereas I had heard female voices singing.

Robert Fripp was the founder of King Crimson. He must have had a similar experience at the Temple of Karnak. I contacted him by e-mail and told him my story, but his manager replied and said that he was not interested. I don't think Robert Fripp even got the letter.

I eventually composed an Egyptian CD called, Ancient Sun with the Goddess Hathor melody I heard that day. The song is called "RA."

The next morning we proceeded to Dendara to the Temple of the Goddess Hathor. This temple was completely different from all the others.

Hathor Temple of Dendera—Photo by Devara ThunderBeat

In the main temple, it felt like a transportation chamber. There is a painting of 12 Zodiac signs and the Sirius star system on the ceiling.

That afternoon we flew back to Cairo and checked into the Mena House. That was the evening our group had private time in the Great Pyramid. I was so excited.

After dinner, the spiritual guide and her fiancé came over to me to say that she would be doing a ceremony in the Great Pyramid that evening and ordered me not to play my drum in the Great Pyramid.

I told her that the main reason I came to Egypt was to play my drum in the Great Pyramid. However, I did not tell her it was to activate the ancient generators below the pyramid to help keep Mother Earth in alignment. I was concerned that she might sabotage the moment.

She then replied "Okay, play your drum after my ceremony, but not during it.

I was not the only one in the group who thought she was mean and dark. Carol the coordinator, received many complaints about her. I definitely did not trust her.

We arrived at the Great Pyramid at 10:00 p.m. The Egyptologist told us that we were allowed to stay until 6:00 a.m. however if anyone wanted to leave before that they could, but could not return to the pyramid.

The first place we went to was the Kings Chamber. There was a granite sarcophagus to the left of the chamber and we all took turns lying inside of it. The length was small. I am 5'5" and anyone taller than that would have to bend their legs. I was surprised it was that small.

While in the sarcophagus, my spirit guides said, "This is an ascension chamber not a tomb, and the Queens Chamber is a healing chamber.

We all sat in a circle for the ceremony in the Kings Chamber. Since I did not trust the spiritual guide, and I had no idea what she had in mind for her ceremony, I visualized a huge protective shield of golden light around me. She did her ceremony.

Everyone then began to leave the Kings Chamber. This was my chance to do the activation for the ancient generators below the pyramid.

I channeled what I was supposed to play on the drum. When I finished, I met up with the group. They were already down in the Queens Chamber. Everyone said they could hear my drum throughout the whole pyramid. "Very good," I said.

In the Queens Chamber, the energy felt much calmer. The Subterranean chambers were next. We went, what seemed to be a long ways down. The Egyptologist said it was an unfinished area. However, what I saw was an ancient city and the pyramid was built on top of it. The stonework looked much older than the rest of the pyramid. There was a walkway going to nowhere and three open rooms to the left. The ancient generators are buried below that.

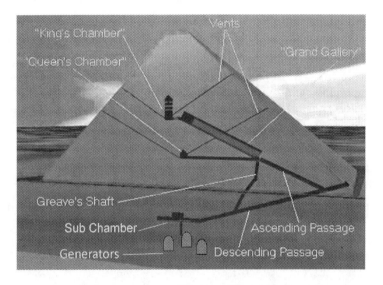

Great Pyramid Inner Diagram by ThunderBeat

After I left the sub-chamber, I was done. I said to the Egyptologist, I am ready to leave the pyramid. He asked if I was tired. "No, not at all, I said, I am finished here."

Carol wanted to leave too, so he guided us out. When we got outside of the pyramid I asked him what time it was, he said it was 4:00 a.m. We had been in there for six hours.

It was still dark outside. We walked a while in the sand when suddenly, I heard the Thunder voice. It said, "Seven is the sacred number, Color, Light, Sound, Seven is the sacred number." He kept repeating this over and over again. I said to myself he is talking about the chakras, the seven rays, the colors of the rainbow, and an activation tone for each chakra.

I became so excited about the information that I wanted to go home right away and compose a Chakra Sound Activation CD. I said to myself, "What, am I crazy? I am in the most unbelievable place in the world, the magical land of Egypt."

I kept thinking about the sacred message and information I had just received. I definitely could not sleep. Okay, there is a musical key for each color and chakra and so on. I put all the information together in my head to develop the Chakra Activational CD. I remembered on the flight to Egypt that I wanted to write a CD with the word Journey in it. That's it! Chakra Journey!

We only had two more days left in Egypt before we fly home.

That evening at dinner, a piano and violin player were performing some beautiful music in the dining area near the lobby. I remembered seeing them before but never got the chance to sit down and listen to them. They were wonderful.

Marilyn mentioned that she would be staying over for a few more days and asked if I would stay and room with her. Carol then said, "If you stay, I have another group coming in a few days, and before they arrive I'd like to take a side trip to Mt. Sinai where they say Moses received the Ten Commandments. Plus, I can give you the trip to Alexandria for free since we had to cancel that trip because our plane was delayed a day."

I said, "Absolutely!" "What a blessing"! I canceled my flight and made plans to stay longer.

Everett stopped by the table and said, "ThunderBeat, I arranged for us to go to the Sphinx and do a meditation between the paws. I want you to come with us."

At that time the Sphinx was under reconstruction and repair and off-limits to the public. We only had a chance to see it at a distance. Of course, I said, I would not miss it for the world!

We met later that evening. Everett had paid a temple guard to guide us to the Sphinx. We had to go over fences and keep very low to the ground so we would not be seen. The temple guard kept watch to make sure that no one was around. I felt like I was in the movie, Mission Impossible. If we were caught, we would go to jail.

Everett was daring and that's what I loved about him. We arrived at the Sphinx and walked into the middle of the paws. At that time, I heard that the sacred tablets were stored inside the left paw. Therefore, the first thing I did was touch the left paw. I instantly heard the male Thunder voice again. He said the Sphinx is from Atlantis. I put my hands up higher on the paw and a huge piece of stone about 2½ feet wide slid off into my hands. The Sphinx was extremely old and falling apart. I had been collecting small rocks from every site I visited, but this was too big to bring home. I pushed it back up to where it belonged and as I did, a small piece from the right corner of the stone slowly rolled *diagonally* down into my left hand. Stones do not fall *diagonally*, they fall straight down. Wow, thank you so much for this gift I said. It even has some fossils in it. I turned around to see what the rest of the group was doing and they were all in meditation. I then joined them in the meditation.

We got back safe with no problems and I thanked Everett and showed him the piece of the Sphinx.

On the last day with the group, we went to the red pyramid, the bent pyramid and the Egyptian Museum. When we got to the museum, I had no idea so many relics had been found in the temples and tombs. They had incredible detailed furniture, jewelry, pottery headdresses and so much more. Amazing!!! The Cairo Museum is so large it would take three days to see everything.

The next morning I went to say my goodbyes to everyone. We were all hugging each other with tears in our eyes. I made some endearing friends. What an incredible journey!

I waved good-bye to everyone on the bus. As I walked back into the hotel lobby, the musicians from the other night were playing and they were playing the theme song from Love Story. I ran outside to see if the bus was still there but it was too late, it was pulling away. My heart melted at that moment as tears rolled down my face. I was wondering why the song from Love Story kept coming to me before I went to Egypt. Now, I know.

The next day Carol rented a driver with a van to take us to Mt. Sinai. It was a two-day journey, crossing over the Suez Canal and into the Sinai Desert.

The first night we stayed over on Aqaba Bay near the mouth of the Red Sea. Carol said she found a place where we could go swimming with the dolphins in the morning.

We settled in for the night and I fell asleep almost immediately.

In the middle of the night, I had to get up to go to the bathroom. I opened my eyes knowing I was in the hotel room, but what I saw was an ancient temple, one I had never seen before. I got off the bed and found myself walking through the temple. There were children playing all around me and I told them I'd be right back. I kept walking towards where I remembered the bathroom was, yet still seeing the temple around me. The children started saying, "Star Fire come back! Star Fire come back!" When I reached the bathroom, I turned on the light, and the temple disappeared. I was definitely in two worlds at the same time. I was hoping to go back to see the temple again, but it was gone. I liked the name the children called me. I wonder where I was. Hmmmm?

It was raining the next day so we didn't go swimming with the dolphins. We then proceeded to Mt. Sinai, which was still another five hours away.

When we arrived at Mt. Sinai, we saw a Greek Orthodox Church on the side of the mountain. We talked to one of the priests who said they believe that this is the mountain where Moses received the Ten Commandments. He did give us some interesting information. He said the original tablets were made of blue sapphire, giving this gem its biblical sacredness, symbolizing truth, loyalty, compassion, and acts as a protector against falsehoods. According to Judaism, sapphire is symbolic of the sky, the heavens and God's throne. In the Old Testament, God's throne is described as a beautiful deep blue, clear stone (Exodus 24:12). This was interesting to me since I am always fascinated with colors, crystals and stones.

We stayed overnight. It was a 3-hour journey by camel up the mountain in the morning at sunrise.

That afternoon, while playing my Doumbek drum outside in the lounge area of the hotel, a man came running over to me and asked if I would play for their belly dancer that evening. I had picked up the Middle Eastern rhythms very quickly.

He said, "You are very good, where are you from?"

"I am from the United States," I said.

"When do you go back?"

"In a few days," I said.

"You stay here, he said. I'll give you a six-month contract to play for my belly dancers."

I laughed, and said, "That is nice, but I cannot stay."

The next morning we went up the mountain by camel. It was slow but steady. Three-quarters of the way up there was a tearoom built inside the mountain. I said, "Hey, this is the original Hard Rock Café." Everyone laughed.

We proceeded up the mountain. When we reached the top, it was beautiful. Marilyn and I looked at each other and said, at the same time, "This is not the place where Moses received the Ten Commandments.

No one really knows on what mountain Moses received the Ten Commandments.

There is the Hebrew version and the Egyptian version about Moses and the Exodus. It is the Egyptian version that most people do not know about.

We got back to Cairo a couple of days before the new group arrived. However, there was a woman Julie, who got there early. She wanted to go see the pyramids before the group arrived. Carol and Marilyn were resting so I took her under my wings.

"We can hire a guide at the horse stables to take us to the Pyramids. During your tour you will be going to the Great Pyramid and I haven't been inside the Middle Pyramid so let's go there."

Julie and I then discussed doing a toning activation meditation in the Queens Chamber.

When we arrived at the stables, the guide with the horses told us that we had only two hours and that it would take a while to get to the pyramids by horse.

When we got to the Middle Pyramid, the guide said, "You don't have much time left." I told him we were only going to be 15 or 20 minutes.

We went into the Queens Chamber, sat down and started toning. A few minutes later, we heard a female voice singing with us. I asked Julie, "Is that you singing that high pitch?" She said, "No, I thought it was you." I said, "No, I can't sing that high."

We continued toning with our eyes closed, and after a few minutes; I felt a tap on my shoulder. It was a man with a Japanese group. He asked if he could take a picture of us. As I nodded yes, I noticed that he appeared to be moving extremely fast, like a movie in high-speed motion.

We finished the short meditation and walked back to our guide. He stood there holding our horses and then began yelling at us. "You said you were only going to be there for 15 minutes. It's been an hour and a half."

Julie and I looked at each other and said how could that be? She looked at her watch and said, "Wow, it has been an hour and a half." We only toned for a few minutes. When we finished our meditation, we thought we had been there for 15 minutes at the most.

I do not know what happened, but time had definitely shifted. That explains why the Japanese group was moving so fast and we heard a woman toning with us with an extremely high pitch that neither one of us could sing. We had shifted into a different dimension of time. I found out later that the Middle Pyramid is a Stargate.

The next day I met the new group and we headed out to the City of Alexandria. I was excited about seeing the Mediterranean Sea. While on the bus, I began writing down my experiences. Before I left on my trip to Egypt, I had a reading from Chief Little Summer. One of the things he said was that I was going to have many magical experiences and that I would forget some of them unless I wrote them down.

We got to Alexandria and it looked like a city in shambles. I was very disappointed. Ramadan was in progress at the time so there were celebrations in the streets. We went to a place where they said it might be Cleopatra's burial chamber. I did not feel that at all.

We ate our lunch at a restaurant that overlooked the Mediterranean Sea. As I looked out at the water, I started naming some of the Greek Islands, names I had never heard before. They just flowed out of my mouth. Since they speak fluent English in Egypt, I asked the waiter if these Islands existed. He said yes and he pointed to the same spot I was talking about. Then I pointed to the left and said, "Over there an island is missing. No one knew what to say. I kept saying there used to be an island there as I pointed to the water.

A year later while watching a program on the History Channel, they had just discovered a sunken island in the Mediterranean Sea off Alexandria. That was exactly the same spot I had mentioned about the missing Island. They had found the remains of Cleopatra's Temple underneath the water, and it was an island that sank from an earthquake about 1000 years ago. It was an Isis temple and was discovered by a Greek Expedition in 1998. I was in Egypt in 1997. They had also found statues of Seti I, father of Ramses II. This dates it back to be a much older temple than Cleopatra's time.

When we got back on the bus, I discovered that all my writings about my journey in Egypt were gone. I asked the Egyptologist and the bus driver but no one had seen them. Hmm, I wondered why someone would take my journal.

We got back to Cairo at the Mena House. Marilyn was leaving the next day, Carol left Cairo with her new group and my flight was leaving in three days. That next evening at dinner, I saw an Egyptian belly dancing show. All the Middle Eastern rhythms the drummers were playing, I was also playing on my drum before I even heard them. I definitely have a connection here.

The next day was my last full day in Egypt. It was another beautiful clear day. During the whole time I had been here, it had not rained in Cairo. For my last day, I decided to take my camera with me and go out on horseback to the pyramids. I so enjoyed riding an Arabian horse in the desert. I had a handsome young guide who kept saying, "Let me take your picture." I said, "Okay, when we get closer to the pyramids."

We went over a large sand dune where I could see the pyramids very well. I put my hands up to the sky and said, "This is ThunderBeat's last day." About five minutes later a huge wall of dark clouds came in from behind the pyramids. A massive storm was heading our way. The guide kept saying let me take your picture and I finally agreed. It started to rain and the horses began to panic so we returned to the stables.

I am so glad he did take that picture otherwise; I would not have gotten this shot. To me, it looks like a Thunder Being or maybe Moses in the clouds right above me.

Face in the clouds—Egypt 1997

When I got home, I immediately began working on the Chakra Journey CD.

I researched and tested the musical notes to activate each chakra. I went through 2500 sounds on my keyboard before I found the right one. I recorded the root chakra, then as soon as I went to record the sacral chakra, Spirit came in and said "NOT YET!" I said "But I am so excited about this project and I have all the information." "NOT YET," the voice said again.

I tried to keep recording but somehow I was stopped. I was also working on a chakra poster and a cover for the CD.

One day I was in a shop in Sarasota, Florida where they had imports from India and I saw this ancient statue. I said, "That is perfect that will be my Chakra CD cover."

I asked the woman about the statue and she said it was a 250 year old, hand carved, wooden statue of Quan Yin and that it had been used in ceremonies for many years. I asked if I could take a picture of it and she said, yes.

When I got back home, I scanned the picture into my computer. While working with it in photo shop, I clicked on the reverse button to show it as a negative. It turned blue and had a white aura around it. I said again, "That's it! That is my CD cover." In 1997, I did not know much about Quan Yin. I researched Quan Yin and this is what I found:

Quan Yin In The Buddhist Tradition. *She is the embodiment of compassionate loving kindness. As the Bodhisattva of Compassion, She hears the cries of all beings. She works with sound to heal and awaken. Quan Yin, as a true Enlightened One, or Bodhisattva, vowed to remain in the earthly realms and not enter the heavenly worlds until all other living things have completed their own enlightenment and thus become liberated from the pain-filled cycle of birth, death, and rebirth.*

I knew that this was the cover for my Chakra Journey CD!

Every six months I would try to record the Chakra Journey CD, but I was stopped by the spirit voice every time. He would say "not yet" It was very frustrating for me.

I purchased some beautiful items when I was in Egypt to sell with my crystals and jewelry. I then arranged for a booth at a UFO conference in Gulf Breeze, Florida. I always wanted to go to Gulf Breeze because it was known as "a hot spot for UFO sightings."

I drove to the conference and set up my table. While there I met a man named Jim, and I had a strong feeling that I knew him, but could not remember from where. It was like seeing a long lost family member that you have not seen for a very long time. I said to him, where do I know you from? He just smiled.

Jim and his mother also had a booth at the conference. He made jewelry. Later that day he made a beautiful necklace for me. He then invited me to his mother's house for dinner and gave me the directions. "Take Route 98 West, go over the bridge and you will see the water then turn right at the end of the bridge, which is my street. It's only 30 minutes away."

Jim left the conference early that day. That evening the conference closed at 8:00 p.m. I called Jim from my cell at 9:00 p.m. and told him I was leaving.

By then it was dark outside.

I got onto Route 98 West. I was driving for a while. There were no side streets or houses anywhere.

I looked at the clock and it was already 10:00 p.m. I called Jim on my cell phone, but could not get any reception. I remembered him saying to go over a bridge you will see the water at the end of the bridge take a right. I went up a ramp and I thought it was a bridge but it was not. I kept driving and driving for miles.

Things started to get really strange. I looked up at the streetlights and I saw orange balls of light, but they didn't have any poles. I was in the middle of the country and I still hadn't seen any houses, buildings or even cars on the road. I kept driving looking for a place to ask for directions, but there was nothing.

I went around a curve and there was a large tree to the right, then the next curve it was the same tree, same curve, and it happened again, same tree same curve. I said out loud, what is going on here? It was now 10:30 p.m. and Jim had said it was only 30 minutes to his house.

I needed to ask somebody for directions. I finally saw a building, it was a greenhouse all lit up. There was a man inside working. He was dressed in white and he looked like a professor working in a lab. I thought, I'll stop here and ask for directions, but there was no driveway to pull into.

I continued driving. I drove a little further and found a bar with a lit "Open" sign and a large parking lot that was empty. I saw a pay phone outside; I tried the pay phone but that did not work.

A car with their top down went by with four people in it laughing. The laughter seemed to echo everywhere and I felt as though I was inside a dome and in a "Twilight Zone" movie. What is going on!

I decided to go into the bar to ask for directions. There were fifteen people inside, yet there were no cars in the parking lot and no houses anywhere that I saw. Hmm, where did they all come from?

There was a horseshoe shaped bar inside and every seat was taken. Two men were standing in the middle of the bar talking. Their conversation was about Quantum Physics. I thought to myself they are probably from the UFO Conference. There was a woman behind the bar so I went up and asked her where the bridge was. I pointed in the direction I came from and asked, "Is it back this way?"

Everyone turned around and shook their heads up and down all at the same time, "Yes." I thanked them, and as I walked out of the bar, I heard one person say, "Do you think she knows where she is?"

"No, I said to myself. That is why I came in here to ask for directions."

I found out later that was not what they meant.

I went back towards the direction I came in from, and less than a mile, I saw the bridge. I wondered how I could have missed this bridge?

I saw the street that I was supposed to go down. I said let me see how long this bridge is. I drove across the bridge and it was at least 30 car lengths. The moon was almost full so I could see the water clearly. How did I miss this bridge? I turned back around and went down Jim's street. I found his house and he came out and said, "Come on in!"

"I'm so sorry I'm late,"

"No worries! Have a seat."

There was a man and a woman sitting at the table. I noticed the woman's eyes were deep and intense. When she looked at me, it was as though she was looking right through me like an x-ray machine. I asked what time it was and Jim said it was a little after midnight. "Wow, it took me a lot longer than 30 minutes to get here," I said. "That's okay, you're here now and that's all that counts," he said.

We all talked for a while then the woman mentioned about an island she lives on. She said, "We would like you to come and live on our island."

I looked at her surprisingly and asked, "What kind of things do you do on this island?"

She then became very short with her words. "Work," she said.

"How many people are on this island?" She said 5,000

"You can have relationships on the island." Then she pointed to her fiancé and said, "I met him on the island."

I then took a deep look at her fiancé and I realized he looked exactly like one of the people from the bar. How can that be? I said to myself.

I said, "Jim, have you been on this island?" He nodded, "yes." Hmm.

I said No to the offer and said I have other plans I want to do with my life.

It did cross my mind that the island they were talking about was a spaceship, but I did not say anything. The couple left and it was getting late. Jim said, "You can stay here and sleep on the couch tonight." "You've been through a lot; you need to get some rest. I'll wake you in the morning."

The next day was Sunday and the last day of the conference. I drove back to the conference in the morning and made sure to keep my eye on the clock. Sure enough, it was only 30 minutes to get there. What happened last night I do not know, but I was definitely missing time. For many years, I kept trying to figure out what really happened that night.

I returned to Sarasota Sunday evening. The next few days the feeling of being pregnant was strong. Then after a few days, I noticed when I was driving I was being followed again. Hmmm???

MORE STRANGE THINGS

The rest of that year, I was performing with a band in the evenings and teaching drum lessons during the day. After our gigs, I always felt energized. Therefore, when I got home at 3:00 a.m. I could not sleep. I would stay up and read for hours. I was studying the Keys of Enoch at that time.

During that time, I started to hear footsteps walking around the outside my house, but I did not see anyone, my outside sensor lights didn't go on and Sheba did not growl.

At times, I would hear knocking on my walls, and when I turned the TV on, I would hear deep mumbling voices underneath the TV program. This was happening for months. One night I heard a loud voice in my living room call my dog's name, Sheba. Sheba even looked up and around the room.

In the mornings when I awakened, I would hear the sounds of a phone ringing in the ceiling above my bed. This happened many times. I checked the attic but nothing was there.

One night when I turned on the TV I heard a deep male voice saying, "You must die now." I was fed up with all the noises and voices so I stepped into my power and said, "What is your name?" He told me his name; however, I could not pronounce it. I never heard this name before. Therefore, I wrote it down. I researched the name in many places, but did not come up with anything. His name was *Mephistopheles.*

I am so glad Sheba was with me. She is a great protector so I always felt safe.

Ask and You Shall Receive

One day when Sheba was outside barking, I said aloud, "I would like to know what my dog is saying."

The next morning when I awoke, Sheba was outside barking and I understood exactly what she was saying. I could hear her in English.

She was saying, "I told you to stay out of the yard. Now, go!"

A few minutes later a loud sound went through my head, "Buzz,-zip!" and then I could no longer understand what Sheba was saying.

Something similar happened about a week later.

In the morning when I woke up, I heard voices coming from my carport, which was right next to my bedroom. I wondered what all those people were doing there.

There was a lot of chattering going on.

I quickly tuned into one of the voices to hear what they were talking about, and I heard, "Don't go over there. I already went over there, there is nothing over there." I then realized it was the birds talking and I could understand them. A few minutes later the "Buzz, zip" sound returned and I could not understand them anymore. I only heard their chirping.

I remembered reading in Chief Little Summer's book about Native Americans hundreds of years ago, who could understand what the animals were, saying. He said they would communicate freely. I presume that is what he was talking about.

One day when I was ready to go jogging, I walked out the door and the Thunder voice came again. He told me to go down the street to the right of my house. I never liked to go that way because I always felt strange energy in that area. I listened to the voice and I said Okay.

When I got to the second block, I saw about ten baby Ibis birds. They were digging in the dirt with their long beaks. I said, Wow, those are little baby Thoth birds. I enjoyed watching them as they ate. I then looked around for their mother, but I didn't see her. I said aloud, "Where is your mother?" Then I heard the Thunder voice say, "Look down". I looked down at my feet and to the left I saw her lying on the ground. She was not moving. When I touched her she was still warm, but she was not alive. I picked her up and gave her a blessing. I told her not to worry about her babies that they will be fine. Then I told her to go to the Light.

I brought her home smudged her and clipped her wings. Today, I still have her wings on the wall above my altar. The symbol for Thoth is the Ibis bird. I felt that this was definitely a sign and gift from Thoth. Thoth is an Ascended Master.

If you pay attention to nature, messages will come to you.

1998

One morning when I woke up, I felt this cone-shaped energy coming through the top of my head. (Crown Chakra) It was a strong buzzing energy. A male voice said, "Your number is 202-20-30." This deity's voice sounded different from the other voices I have heard.

I wrote down the number and it looked like a phone number. I called the number, but no such number. I did some research and the only thing that I found with that sequence of numbers was in the book, The Keys of Enoch.

The 202-20-30 section of the book talks about the DNA-RNA and the light codes, and the 22 Hebrew fire letters, which are thought forms of light vibration. The thought forms are also coordinated with sound harmonics, musical notes. I said to myself "very interesting". I didn't completely understand it then. It took me 15 years to realize why I received the message and the numbers.

One other time I was lucid dreaming, but this dream continued when I opened my eyes. I saw myself in a small, square silver spaceship and we were headed towards Earth. A voice was saying, "We are taking you back to Earth now". They dropped me off in a city that I didn't know. I even remember asking them why they were dropping me off in a place I did not live. It was an empty parking lot with buildings on one side, and a bridge above me with cars going over it. There were many people walking through the parking lot. Then this vision vanished. I stored all that into my memory bank for later.

I was performing with a band at a three-day outdoor festival in Kansas. We drove there and set up camp. On the second night, a girl from the festival I never met before came up to me and said, "I am supposed to bring you up to the top of the mountain. We call it Gaia Mountain", which means Mother Earth.

"Who told you to bring me there?" I said.

"Spirit told me. It is the place where sacred ceremony is held. You can do a ceremony there if you like," she said.

"Is anyone else up there doing ceremony?"

"No, not just anyone is allowed there, you are supposed to go there by yourself."

I followed her as she led me up the mountain. When we got there she said, "I'll meet you on the lower level when you're done to guide you back down the mountain."

I looked around and saw a beautiful, large tree with a spiraling pathway in front of it. I followed the pathway and gave a blessing to Mother Earth, I prayed for more Love on the Earth. About 30 minutes later, I started to walk down the mountain. The girl was waiting for me at the next level of the mountain ridge. She asked me if I had done a ceremony. Yes, I said I gave a blessing to Mother Earth. Then she stopped and looked at me and said you look very different. "I do?" I said.

I then walked down the mountain out to a ledge at the middle of the mountain. Darkness had fallen and I saw the moon coming out from behind some dark clouds. I did feel different I felt very powerful. I even felt my clothes were different as if I had an animal's fur on. I picked up a long piece of wood along the way and it felt like a staff.

I put my right hand up to the clouds then suddenly, thunder rolled across the sky. I said, wow, did I do that? Then I put my left hand out and waved it across the clouds and rolling thunder happened again. It happened three times in a row. I remembered my ThunderBeat past-life reading with the psychic in San Francisco saying that I could put my hand up to the clouds and rolling thunder would happen. Another girl came up to me that I knew and said wow you look like a completely different person. I don't know how the transfer happened on top of the mountain, but I do know that when you do ceremony blessings and prayers for the people and the Earth, a major shift takes place in your body, mind, and spirit heart.

It was getting late so I walked down to my tent. Later that evening it gently rained and I didn't hear any thunder sounds at all.

We performed the next night, and the next day I was ready to drive home. I never did see the girl again that lend me up the Mountain.

On the drive back I felt a strong 'pull' to go to New Orleans. I had never been there before, but I knew I was supposed to go to the French Quarter. I had heard many things about this place. Therefore, I followed my intuition.

One of the band members was with me. When we arrived, we parked the car and walked around. About 30 minutes later, I began to recognize people. It was as though I knew them, but I could not remember from where. There was over a dozen people that I recognized. I even looked right at them to see if they recognized me, but they did not.

I then walked into a coffee shop to get some coffee for the drive home. There was a group of men sitting around a table. One man was talking and then they all turned around and looked at me. The man that was talking said to the group, "Oh, she's a drummer." I have no idea how he knew that. I did not recognize him or anyone one in his group, but he recognized me.

As we drove out of New Orleans, I saw the bridge and the parking lot where the spaceship dropped me off in the lucid dream I had. There it was, In New Orleans. Hmmmm?

As I was driving out of town, I saw a few more people I felt I knew. I had strongly been drawn to go there and yet, I did not know why. I did recognize many people there. I felt as though I was in a twilight zone movie again. Hmm, this was one more thing to store in my wonderment bank for later.

MAYAN JOURNEY

Ever since I had that reading with Delfina Rose, I wanted to go to the Mayan lands.

In 1998, I met a couple who told me about a shaman who was taking a group down to the Mayan lands on the Spring Equinox. This is the time when the sun hits the "Kukulcan Pyramid" at Chichen Itza and the shadow of the snake comes down the side of the pyramid. The shaman planned a journey to Chichen Itza and many other Mayan temples. I was excited because of the reading I had with Delfina Rose when she said that I was once a Mayan High Priestess a thousand years ago. I wanted to see if I would recognize any of the temples.

We met at the shaman's house in Ft. Lauderdale, Florida. There were 12 of us in the group. We flew into Merida where we rented some cars, and then drove to Chichen Itza. We got there the day before the Equinox, March 20, and at least 3,000 people were there at that time. The shaman said it was best to go the day before because 7,000 to 10,000 people show up for the Spring Equinox every year and it would be difficult going through many of the temples.

When we arrived, we were told we were not allowed to climb any of the temples or pyramids. Some of the main places were roped off. I said to a girl from the group who was standing next to me, "I didn't come this far to not be able to touch and experience the pyramid. See that doorway on the side of the pyramid? I am going inside there. Watch my back!"

When I got inside the doorway, there were no lights. It was completely dark, so I 'looked' through my third eye in order to see. I saw a stairway and looked up the stairs. All of a sudden, six ETs came running down the stairs, five were gray and one was pink. They had large dark eyes. They said to me without speaking verbally, (mental telepathy) "You cannot be in here, you have to leave now."

They seemed very nervous, almost in a panic that I was in there. I was not afraid, I said, "Okay, I am leaving." I backed out of the doorway and went behind the rope. The girl that was watching my back said, "Where did you come from? I didn't see you come back out of the doorway, and when you started walking towards it, you disappeared before you got there. I said I must have become invisible because I didn't want to be caught, otherwise I'd go to jail. She asked me what was in there. I told her there were gray ETs who told me to leave and that I felt they were up to something because they were very nervous when they saw me in there.

I found out later at the top of the stairs inside the pyramid, there is a Jaguar altar where they did ancient ceremonies. Now, why would the grays be in there during the spring equinox? Hmmm.

We proceeded to walk around the temple grounds and then came up to an Ancient observatory. This area was not roped off so I was excited to go inside. As I walked up the stairway a police officer said, "If you go any further I will take you to jail. "We were not even allowed to walk close to it. Something was going on.

That afternoon we went to Uxmal. This place was very interesting.

Uxmal *was the greatest religious center in the Puuc Hills of Yucatan, flourishing between the 7th and 10th centuries A.D. Central to the ruin site is the great **Pyramid of the Magician**, that carries a tale.*

Legend has it that a new king would come to rule the city when a magical "gong" was sounded in the nearby jungle. One day such a sound was heard in the surrounding hills and a dwarf magician-god from the sky named **Itzamna** *appeared in the city. The City-King, not ready to give up the realm to a stranger, ordered the young "God" executed, but among the villagers forced the king to issue the dwarf-boy a challenge. The king agreed the boy could live and become king if he could construct a grand pyramid overnight.*

Confident he had saved his ruler ship and kingdom, the Maya lord slept soundly through the night, only to rise the next morning to witness the appearance of a huge pyramid, the **Pyramid of the Magician**, *which the dwarf apparently had built with his magic in a single night.*

This structure was a school for the training of healers, astronomers, mathematicians, shamans, priest and high priestesses. It was an ancient and ongoing use as a mystery school and ceremonial center. It is also interesting to note that the entire city is aligned with the planets and with Venus predominating, and that the pyramid of the magician is oriented so that its stairway on the west faces the setting sun at the time of summer solstice.

Uxmal Temple of the Magician—Photo by Devara ThunderBeat

Our shaman guide said this is where the High Priestesses were trained. I wonder if this was the place, Delfina Rose was taking about. She said I spent my younger years completing the 33 steps of knowledge to be a High Priestess and that most people did not complete all the steps.

We were there for a couple of hours and I walked everywhere. I climbed the Pyramid of the Magician, but still did not feel anything. There was another pyramid called the Grand Pyramid with McCaw birds carved on the top of it. I also climbed that one. I felt very peaceful there but I did not recognize anything. I felt very disappointed.

That night we stay at a hotel very close to Uxmal. It was sunset, and when I looked out from my hotel balcony, I could see the site in the distance. That is when I received a stunning vision. I saw myself standing on the Grand Pyramid, the one with the birds carved on it and I was being initiated. I had a white dress on with long bell sleeves. My hair was black with bangs and I almost looked exactly like my picture on the cover of this book. I was wearing a headband. A male shaman was initiating me. He was very handsome with long, black hair. The colors he was wearing were turquoise and red. In Native American culture, those colors mean earth and sky. During the initiation, in front of the pyramid was a courtyard with hundreds of people standing there, and they were all cheering. Yeah!!!

The vision was so clear to me, and it confirmed what Delfina Rose had said. Uxmal was a school. So where was I from and where did I live after my training? It was several years later before I had these questions answered.

It was when I had the Akashic Records reading with Lisa Barnett.

During the past life reading, I did not tell Lisa about my vision from Uxmal or about the reading with Delfina Rose. However, I did ask her if I had any Mayan past lives. She said yes. She said I was born in Belize.

The people in Belize needed a High Priestess. I was chosen. She said they took me at the age of five to a school to become a High Priestess and that I remained there until I was twenty-five. According to Lisa, I completed all of the steps needed become a High Priestess. I returned to Belize where I served as the High Priestess in the community up to my late nineties. My name was Amara. Now I know why I always felt a longing for Belize and a knowing I did not live in Uxmal for my whole life.

During our journey, our shaman guide was talking highly about a man named John Major Jenkins. We were to meet up with him to join the group for the rest of the journey. He is an author and independent researcher, best known for his works with astronomical and esoteric connections of the calendar systems used by the Maya civilization. He talked about the Mayan Calendar and the date, December 21, 2012. At that time, he had just finished writing his book "Maya Cosmogenesis 2012," which was still being edited by his publisher.

He was a very scientific man with a big heart and full of incredible knowledge. I got a chance to pick his brain. I also told him that I could tune into the energies of a place, ask for information, and download the knowledge ethereally.

Every evening after dinner, our group got together and we shared our experiences with each other. By the third evening, John Major Jenkins said to me, "You have answered about a dozen questions I had. I wish I met you before I finished my book." I told him that he could use my information in his next book if he wanted to.

The next day we met up with a Mayan elder named Hunbatz Men. We did a ceremony with him and his group of 70 people at the Cenote healing waters near Chichen Itza. In Mexico, ceremonies are not allowed as you have to get permission and even then, the police are watching you. After that, we went swimming in the healing waters.

That evening we went to a conference with many Elders speaking about the Mayan Prophecies. John Major Jenkins and Hunbatz Men were speaking there, too.

The next day we drove many hours to a deep cave. We met up with a man who was the guide for the cave. He planned to do a ceremony, but indicated that we had to go deep inside the cave so no one could see us. My spirit guides told me to give some of my crystals to him, and so I did. I said, "These are for you, you will need them." He said that he did not need them because he had his own. However, I insisted that he take them, and told him that they were a gift, so he did.

About an hour later, we were deep inside the cave. He said this is where we will do the ceremony. He took out his crystals, but some of them were gone. He looked all over the ground for a while. He then looked at me and said, "How did you know?"

"I did not know you lost some crystals, Spirit just told me to give them to you."

He went back towards the entranceway looking for his crystals. He was gone for about 15 to 20 minutes. When he returned he looked at me with an angry look on his face like it was my fault.

"Did you find your crystals?" I asked. He shook his head 'no', then said," I have had those crystals for many years and they were very sacred to me."

I said, "All I know is that spirit said to give you some crystals because you will need them".

We all did the ceremony together, but I could feel he was still very upset. On the walk out of the cave, I reassured him again that it was Spirit that told me to give some of my crystals to him. John Major Jenkins was amazed that I knew to give him the crystals. He said he wanted to learn how to do that. I started to teach John how to feel energies.

We set out the next day under clear blue skies for Campeche to a place called Edzna. When I heard the name of the temple, I remembered there was a place in Egypt called Edsna. When I checked the world map, I discovered that they were on the same gridline. Edzna ended up being one of my favorite temples. When we arrived, we had the whole place to ourselves.

The great pyramid at Edzna was called the Temple of the Sun. I climbed up to the top and went inside the large chamber. There was a circle— shaped stone embedded at the doorway and two other chambers inside. When I went inside the one chamber to the right, I instantly felt as though I was being pulled upwards. Then I walked inside the other chamber on the left and I felt like I was being pulled downwards. I then stood in the doorway on the circle of stone, and an alignment occurred between Heaven and Earth. Then I heard the Thunder Voice. He said "Go down to the side of the temple."

When I reached the bottom of the pyramid, one of the women from the group asked me what I felt about Edzna. "Spirit said to go to the side of the pyramid," I said. She then asked if she could come with me and I told her yes she could. Usually I like to walk alone so I would not be distracted by other people's energy. It is easier for me to receive messages and information that way.

When I got to the side of the temple, I said, "Okay, I am here."

I looked up and suddenly a rainbow appeared from the clear blue sky. I watched it come down and hit the top of the pyramid and whole pyramid turned into rainbow iridescent colors and was surrounded by golden light that glowed. I said, "That is Atlantis and the Golden City of Light, how beautiful."

The woman kept looking up and I asked her if she could see the rainbow. She said, "No, but I believe you." I said, now I know what the Mayans were talking about when they said, "We have cities made of gold." They were talking about the golden light.

I continued to walk around the site to other structures in the courtyard. I asked Spirit for the ancient ceremony music and I was shown a vision of the temple next to the Pyramid of the Sun. The vision was inside this temple. They showed me colored lights spinning around very fast, and the sound I heard was like a high-pitched didgeridoo. Spirit said these are the Galactic activation tones, which brings you into higher dimensions of light. The girl was still with me I pointed at the temple and said, "This temple is a sound, light, color healing chamber." I was also shown a vision of the instrument making the sound I heard. It was a long, wooden stringed instrument. The galactic sounds I heard that day I recorded onto my "Mayan Landing CD"

The next day we went to Palenque Temple, tomb of Pacal Votan. Associations of Votan and Palenque have led spiritual leader José Argüelles to identify Pacal the Great as "Pacal Votan" and to identify himself as an incarnation of "Valum Votan" as his son.

José Argüelles—was best known as the initiator of the world famous Harmonic Convergence global peace meditation, which occurred on August 16-17, 1987. During that time, he also awakened the mass consciousness to the significance of the year 2012 and turned the world's attention toward the Maya and their calendric system. His bestselling book, "The Mayan Factor" (1987) gives credence to the Mayan Calendar's cycles of natural time, and reveals the historically unprecedented galactic shift in time coming in 2012. José Argüelles is also recognized as one of the creators of the Earth Day concept and founder of the Whole Earth Festival.

One of the temples looks like it is from China. The message I 'received' was that "Pacal Votan" was a bringer of light with messages from the stars. We spent the whole day there. It was a very peaceful day.

We went to Agua Azul and Miso-Ha falls and then headed back to Merida to stay for the night.

The next day we all went out for lunch. On the way, I saw a store that I wanted to go into, but it was closed. I felt very drawn to go inside. I said to myself, I am supposed to go into that store. Although I could not see too much inside, I did notice a few Mayan items in the front window. I just knew I had to go inside.

It was still closed the next day, but the following day when we were leaving, it was open. I asked everyone if they could please wait as I would only be a minute. When I walked into the store, the owner was talking to a man. There were ancient relics from the Mayan temples in that store and I found out that it was only open by appointment.

I was first drawn to a crystal. When I put it up to the light, I could see Jesus, Mary Magdalene and two children inside of it. It was not carved, it was natural and very detailed. I asked how much it was, but I didn't have enough money with me. My money was in my suitcase and was buried with everyone else's. However, I did purchase a different crystal. When I brought it up to the counter, the man said, "You are a healer?" I told him I was. He said the crystal wand was used by Ancient Mayan shamans for healing. It was not quartz crystal, but was made of golden calcite. The energy from it was very powerful.

One of the women in our group had been having back pain for days. I put the crystal on her back and ran some of my Reiki energy through it. In less than five minutes, the pain had gone. She said that was amazing. I told her to let me know if she needed me to do this again. A few days went by and I asked her how her back was. She said she still had no pain. To this day, I still use that crystal in my personal healing sessions.

When I got home from the Mayan Lands, I started writing some tribal music. Six or seven songs came out very quickly. I did not know the names of the songs until later. I became very busy with other things so I put them aside for a while. A few months later when I listened back to them, I knew instantly what the names of the songs were: The Jaguar Speaks, Galactic Voyage, The Feathered Serpent, Jungle Talk, and Ceremony. I also channeled in the Jaguar. I prayed to him for three days and asked him to give me a message from the Jaguar family. On the third day of asking, he gave me this message.

THE JAGUAR SPEAKS

We walk gently upon the Earth
Gracefully with every step we take
You destroy the jungle and the plants that give you life
Not till you understand the meaning of life
Will you understand the Jaguar
Without the Jaguar, humans cannot exist.

This song and message ended up being on my Mayan Landing CD, too.

Chapter 3

ACTIVATION

THE RED ROCKS OF SEDONA

Sedona, Arizona—Photo by Devara ThunderBeat

In 1999, my friends asked me, what is the next sacred site you are going to? I said that I hadn't been drawn to any place yet. They said why don't you go to Sedona, Arizona. I said Sedona? I've never heard of it. They said what? Sedona is totally your energy. It is a very spiritual place and a lot of Native American culture is there. That was all they told me.

In June, we flew into Phoenix and drove up to Sedona. I saw the Red Rocks for the first time and I noticed that everyone kept looking at me for my reaction. I saw that one of the rock formations had a huge golden glow around it. I said, "Wow, this is the Ancient city of golden light." We drove a few more miles and then I said, "Sedona used to be under water. They said, "Yes, it was."

"The water is deep, and it was about three quarters of the way up the rocks. I also see large boats sailing in the waters and up above were flying baskets with sails." They were floating like balloons but the sails were just like sails on a boat so they had to be powered in some different way. I was in awe of the beauty of this place. It was breathtaking.

We hiked in the Red Rocks and I did a ceremony honoring Mother Earth. I felt the Vortexes they talk about. I kept telling the girls about the UFO clouds. There are UFOs hiding in clouds that they create. I would see them all the time in Florida. One girl asked, "Where are they?" I said, "I'll point one out to you as soon as I see one."

A few days later, we took a ride up to Hopi Land, one of the oldest Native American tribes remaining in the USA. It was about a 2—hour drive from Sedona. About an hour into the ride, I saw a UFO Cloud. I pointed and said, "There is a UFO Cloud, and I know for a fact it is one because there are three black helicopters hovering on the side of the cloud." It was a big one. The girls got very quiet and seemed nervous.

"Do you see it?" I asked.

"Yes, is that what they look like?"

"Yes, I replied. They are everywhere. You just have to look up."

We watched it and the helicopters for about 20 minutes. We then turned north and couldn't see the cloud anymore.

When we got to the Hopi Land late in the afternoon, I bought some beautiful turquoise jewelry. All the tourists had to leave, but I said let's stay. We walked around some more and saw they were having a Kachina dance. It was a star kachina dance. They are not open to the public. A native woman from the tribe looked at me and said, "Come sit over here." The girls didn't want to intrude so they stayed outside by the doorway. I felt honored.

KACHINA

*A kachina is a spirit being in western Pueblo cosmology and religious practices. The western Pueblo, Native American cultures located in the southwestern United States, include Hopi, Zuni, Tewa Village (on the Hopi Reservation), Acoma Pueblo, and Laguna Pueblo. The term also refers to the **kachina dancers**, masked members of the tribe who dress up as kachinas for religious ceremonies, and kachina dolls, wooden figures representing kachinas which are given as gifts to children.*

Kachinas are spirits or personifications of things in the real world. A kachina can represent anything in the natural world or cosmos, from a revered ancestor to an element, a location, a quality, a natural phenomenon, or a concept. There are more than 400 different kachinas in Hopi and Pueblo culture. The local pantheon of kachinas varies in each pueblo community; there may be kachinas for the sun, stars, thunderstorms, wind, corn, insects, and many other concepts. Kachinas are understood as having humanlike relationships; they may have uncles, sisters, and grandmothers, and may marry and have children and are connected with the Fifth World. Each is viewed as a powerful being who, if given honor and respect, can use their particular power for human good, bringing rainfall, healing, fertility, or protection.

"The central theme of the kachina [religion] is the presence of life in all objects that fill the universe. Everything has an essence or a life force, and humans must interact with these or fail to survive."

It was still daylight when we headed back to Sedona. Sue was driving. While driving through the Navaho reservation we passed a man in a truck, and what I saw in his passenger seat, was an ET. I saw it plain as day. The ET was all white with big dark eyes and he was bouncing around in the truck. I wondered if they picked him up from the UFO Cloud ship, we saw earlier.

We only had a few days left in Sedona and I was already missing it. I felt like I was home. I had never felt that way in any place I lived or traveled to even in Egypt or the Mayan lands where I have had past lives.

When I got back home to Sarasota, I was playing with two different bands at that time. Both bands were constantly arguing among themselves. The guitar player in one of the bands was extremely mean to me. I was very disappointed with both of them because they talked spiritually, but were not walking their talk.

I was writing new songs on my own and one night Spirit said to me to go solo. I said, "What? How does a drummer go solo?" He said, "Go solo NOW!"

I thought about it and said, Yes, I am tired of all the arguing in the bands and I am tired of Sarasota. Right then and there, I made up my mind to move to Sedona, Arizona.

Although I was under contract with one of the bands and just finishing a CD with them, I gave them my three months' notice. Everyone said, "Are you crazy? You are in the best bands in the State of Florida." I said, "It's time for me to go."

At that time, my mom wasn't doing well and she wanted to move into a retirement home. I said okay. I knew she would be taken care of and this gave me my freedom to move. I had been in Florida for nine long years.

I was still hearing weird noises—footsteps walking around my house, knocking on my walls, phones ringing in my ceiling and evil voices coming through the TV. I mentioned this to a few friends, but no one seemed to know what it could be.

In February 2000, I packed up everything, rented out my house, and rented a U-Haul. I was on my way to Sedona. I didn't know anyone there. This was a new chapter in my life.

On the way to Sedona, I stopped in New Orleans and went to the French Quarter for lunch. I wanted to see if I recognized anyone again.

As I was walking around a man came up to me and tried to sell me his book. He kept repeating, "You are supposed to have this book." I kept on walking and he started to follow me. There were many people walking around so I felt safe. He proceeded to say, "If the government found out about me writing this book I would be put in jail." I stopped and looked at him and took a look at the book. It was called, "An Alien Conversation about the Chariot of God." It had a lot of sacred geometry symbols and information about ETs. He said again, you are supposed to have this book. I said, okay, and purchased the book from him.

At that time in New Orleans, I didn't recognize anyone like I did when I was there before, but that one guy with his book seemed to recognize me. I left New Orleans and continued on to Sedona.

When I arrived in Sedona, I booked a hotel room for a few days. The first night I was exhausted from all the driving, so I ordered room service. A man came to the door with my food and in a hostile voice said, "This should hold you for a while."

The food knocked me out for two days. I think somebody was still following me and trying to slow me down. I do not know why.

After a few days, I found a house to rent. After being in the new house for only a week, I woke up one morning at 3:00a.m. I felt the whole house vibrating, and I knew it was a spaceship over my house. It happened three times and always at 3:00a.m. within a three-week period.

On the third time, there was a tree near my bedroom window and they came so close to the house that I heard the tree break. I was mad. I started yelling at them saying, "Look what you've done, you broke the tree. I am trying to get some sleep. Now, leave me alone!" The next day I went outside to look at the tree and the whole top of it was broken over.

After a month had gone by, the weird sounds started happening again—the footsteps walking around my house, knocking on my walls, phones ringing in my ceiling and the evil voices coming through my TV. I said to myself, I am in Sedona now and this is supposed to be a spiritual place. There has to be somebody that understands what I am experiencing and can help me.

One day a new sound came into my house. The best way to describe it, was a flute player playing fast. It happened a few times and one day it even followed me into the grocery store. I was standing in one of the aisles when I heard a loud shrieking flute sound. I happened to be standing next to a woman. I asked her, "Did you hear that?" She said, "Hear what?" I said, "It sounded like a flute player." She said no. I guess I was the only one that could hear it. I found out later it was a Kokopelli. Here is the legend of the Kokopelli.

kokopelli

Kokopelli's *usual noisy announcement upon arrival secured both the identity, and therefore the safety, of his unique presence. Kokopelli is a fertility deity, usually depicted as a flute player (often with feathers or antenna-like protrusions on his head), who has been respected by some Native American cultures in the Southwestern United States. Like most fertility deities, Kokopelli presides over both childbirth and agriculture. He is also a trickster god and represents the spirit of music.*

I finally told the deity to go away and he did.

The first people I met in Sedona were a group of musicians. They were spiritual and a lot of fun. I told them about the man I met in New Orleans and showed them the book. They said, "We know him we were wondering if he finished his book". "He used to live in Sedona". They looked through the book and said, "Hey both of us are in the book, look here are our names". "We always wondered what happened to him". "He would always say he was being followed around by the government". They both noticed it was written a while ago and said it is safe now to reveal this information. The book was a creation story about ETs and humans on Planet Earth, and the flower of life. Since the book contained some of their information, I gave them the book.

It was very interesting that the first people I meet in Sedona knew of the man I met in New Orleans. I never told him that I was going to Sedona, and he never asked me. Hmmm! No coincidence here.

I still needed to know what the voices and the knocks and weird things were about. There were a lot of healers and psychics in this town. Surely, someone had to know what was going on. I kept asking people, but no one seemed to have a clue. All they kept telling me was "if you're not supposed to be in Sedona, Sedona will kick you out." Deep inside, I felt that I was supposed to be in Sedona. This place felt more like home then any place I have been.

I wanted to get out of the house that I was renting. With all the weird things happening, I was becoming afraid. I had given the property owner a two months security deposit and a month's rent, which was most of my money. I told the property owner about the strange things that were going on and asked him for my deposit back. He said he spent it, but could give me a little of it every month. I said, "Now, what am I going to do?" I don't have enough money to rent another place.

A few days later I met a woman at a music gathering and told her that I had to get out of the place I was renting because of the weird things that were happening. She said that she was going out of town for a few months and that I could move into one of her houses. All I had to pay were the utilities. She had a few houses in Sedona. The next day she showed me her place to see if I would like to stay there. She said the backyard is all fenced in for your dog.

When we got there, it looked like a mansion. It was extremely private and had a Jacuzzi in the back. Wow, what a blessing! I knew that I was supposed to be in Sedona. She gave me her place for four months. I moved in at the end of the month. I set up my recording studio and wrote my first solo CD, called "Fly High." This CD is a musical journey about my ET experiences.

After I moved into the new place, I finally met someone who had gone through a similar situation of strange happenings as I did. She said, "You need to go and see this shaman. He will know what to do." She actually made the appointment on the phone for me while I was at her house.

During the session with the shaman, he said, "Tell me what's going on." I told him as much as I could understand. I even told him the evil entity's name but he said he never heard the name before. He looked at me and asked, "Does it seem like you're having poltergeist?"

I said, "Yes, that makes so much sense I never thought of that".

We talked for a while. He then proceeded to describe a woman who was a member of one of the bands I was with in Florida. He started laughing and said, "The girl you thought was spiritual put 50 hexes on you. That is why you are having poltergeist. She kept repeating the hex because she did not see you being affected by them. You also have four ET implants from four different races. You are going to need two sessions." "Why would someone do something so evil?" I said. "She was jealous of you. Jealousy is more evil then people realize. People do cruel things including murder because of jealousy."

Here is some information about poltergeist.

Poltergeist—from Wikipedia

In paranormal studies, a poltergeist is the apparent manifestation of an invisible but noisy, disruptive or destructive entity. Most accounts of poltergeist manifestations involve noises and destruction that have no apparent cause. Reports also include inanimate objects being picked up and thrown as if by an invisible person; noises such as knocking, rapping, or even human voices;

Poltergeists have traditionally been described as troublesome spirits who, unlike ghosts, haunt a particular person instead of a specific location. Such alleged poltergeist manifestations have been reported in many cultures and countries including the United States, Japan, Brazil, Australia, and most European nations. The earliest recorded cases date back to the 1st century.

He started removing the hexes with the first session. He said, "As I remove these hexes they will return to her, she will think that you have done something to her, but it is her own curses going back to her."

In the middle of the session, I heard the evil voices swearing and cursing at me. The shaman said he did not hear them.

I found out years later that the girl who put the hexes on me could not write any songs or perform for two years. Several people told me she did not even want to come out of her house, even though she was a very social person.

The next session was the removal of the implants. This shaman man was remarkable. He showed me a five-page outline that he had put together about different ET races, demons and physical deficiencies. He said that all four were etheric implants and none of them was reptilian. It took him about a half hour. I did not feel a thing. There was no pain whatsoever.

That evening after the session about 11:00 p.m., I was getting ready for bed, all of a sudden I felt the house vibrating. I said oh no, not again. Then every ceiling light fixture in the house did a loud electrical pop, one after another. I knew what they were doing, they were looking for me. I called the shaman but there was no answer. I then hid under the covers not knowing what else to do. The popping lasted for about 15 minutes then it stopped. Sheba kept looking at the ceiling. After that occurrence, I never had trouble like that again.

All the strange things that happened to me over the last three years ended. The shaman was a powerful man and I thank God for him every day.

I was still curious about who this Mephistopheles entity was. No one knew until I met Michael.

Michael was a Templar of Knights of the Round Table at St John Vianney's Catholic Church in Sedona. He said, "Mephistopheles is the right-hand man of Satan and he tries to take your soul. We have a whole list with names of Angels and Demons. The Catholic Church has known of these things for centuries."

After that whole experience with hexes and poltergeist, I definitely wanted to learn how to protect myself from dark energies. I heard about a man named John G. Livingston. He is a spiritual counselor, a shamanic exorcist, and is an expert in this field. I contacted him and received the knowledge on how to recognize the dark energies and demons attached to people. He also taught me how to release the dark energies from people and myself. He said The Archangel Michael is a warrior angel and he will help you to dissipate dark entities. This made me feel so much more protected and powerful. He said. "This is more common then people think. Demons are invisible hostile beings sent by the Dark Forces. Their mission is to create fear and chaos, cause destruction, and keep "light workers" from achieving their life purpose." His book is called "Adversaries Walk Among Us." If interested, I highly recommend reading his book.

After that, my days became peaceful. I was composing a lot of music and I finished my "Fly High" CD. One day when I was recording the "Fly High" CD, Jimi Hendrix "came in." His face flashed in front of me. I actually heard him tell me he liked the music and helped me with mixing it. The CD is actually a lot of FUN! It has some words, but is mostly music.

When I finished the CD, I took it to Star Sound Studios to be mastered. The owner's name is Kenny. As we were sitting in the studio together, a flash of blue light came in and the face of Jimi Hendrix appeared on the big piece of glass in the studio. Kenny said, "Did you see that? Jimi Hendrix's face just flashed on the window". I said yes. I proceeded to tell Kenny that Jimi's spirit came into my studio while I was recording this CD. I never told anyone because I thought people would not believe me or think I am crazy. Kenny said, "Well I saw him plain as day". That made me feel really good!

I don't know why Jimi Hendrix came to me. I do remember my first band we played many of his songs and of course, I admire him greatly.

This is one of my favorite quotations from Jimi.

When the power of love overcomes
the love for power, the world will know peace.
—Jimi Hendrix

Sedona and the Red Rocks is a place for hiking. It has hundreds of trails. Sheba and I started hiking two to three times a week.

One week I was drawn to go to Boynton Canyon another magical place in Sedona. On the drive out there, I had to pass a place called Long Canyon. I had to take a left at the Stop Sign to get to Boynton Canyon. Long Canyon is to your right.

Just before the Stop Sign, a white flash covered my car and I was transported into Long Canyon. At that point, my car was in the middle of the road and I was not moving. I thought how did I get here? I remembered the white flash, but this was the opposite way to Boynton Canyon.

I started to turn around and then heard the Thunder Voice.

"Go this way," which meant to stay on the Long Canyon road. Therefore, I turned back around and started driving into Long Canyon. The voice told me where to stop and hike. I parked but could not see any trail, and yet I knew to trust this voice.

After hiking off trail for about 45 minutes, I found a cave and saw an old man spirit inside. He had long, gray hair and a long beard, and wearing a white robe and had a staff in his hand. I bowed, thanked him and continued walking. I got to a large canyon and said, "This looks like an ancient amphitheater." As soon as I said that, I heard thousands of voices cheering. Then I looked around and said this place looks familiar. I must have seen it from the road when I first came to visit Sedona. I found out later you could not see this area from the road. HMMM.

I hiked for about two more hours then went back to the road where my car was. I said to myself, "I am supposed to see something else while I am here."

Thunder Voice came in again and said, "Turn around." I turned around and there it was—a huge sphinx in the rocks. The view to the left and to the right of it was blocked by mountains so one could only see it from where I was standing. I said "Incredible, thank you Great Spirit for showing me this."

SPHINX IN SEDONA—Photo by Devara ThunderBeat

This place called Sedona is so magical and more ancient then people realize. I am discovering there is a lot of ancient Egypt here. My spirit guides told me there are 13 sphinxes. So far, to this day I have found ten.

Later, I talked to the shaman and told him of my experience. He said the cheers I heard in the canyon were my welcoming home. He said why it looked familiar to me was because I had been there before in a past life.

A few days later, I saw a poster for a sound healing gathering with a man named John Dumas, a didgeridoo player. When I looked at his picture, I felt that I knew him from a past life.

I decided to go to his gathering. About 15 people showed up. We all sat on the ground and formed a circle. John played his didgeridoo over each person one at a time. I went into an altered state and I saw myself inside the Mayan sound healing chamber at Edzna, MX. Colored lights were spinning around and the sound of his didgeridoo was echoing off the walls of the temple. It was the same vision I had when I was at that temple. I found out later that John was a Mayan High Priest in a past life and that he was the one who initiated me as a Mayan High priestess a thousand years ago. It is a wonderful feeling when you cross paths with people from your past lives.

I needed to get some income, so I put flyers around town advertising drum lessons. At that time, I still had not met very many people. My first call was from Jesse Kālu, a well-known flute player in the area, asking me to perform with him at a grand opening for The Creative Life Center, a place where conferences and live concerts are held. I said yes. He brought in John Dumas the Didgeridoo player, who I just met a few weeks ago. We hit it off well and wrote ten songs together in one day.

We were all solo artists, so we planned to play together for only the one performance. We called ourselves "One Heart." After our performance, about a dozen people asked us where we would be playing next. We all looked at each other and said; so far, we do not have any plans to perform together again. Everyone said we were wonderful and that we had to play some additional concerts. Again, we looked at each other and said "Okay."

Jesse booked our next performance at an art gallery. A multi award winning music producer Tim Jessup was in the audience. He came up to us after our performance and said we were fantastic and wanted to record us for free. Wow, that was the fastest music opportunity I ever had in my music career. For our third performance together, we recorded a CD and called it "One Heart Live in Sedona." We ended up performing together for two more years. We had a lot of fun and sold thousands of the One Heart CD.

I was still trying to record the Chakra CD, but a Spirit Voice kept saying, not yet. I knew this was a very special healing and awakening CD as I received the color, light, and sound information from being overnight in the Great Pyramid in Egypt. I did not know why they kept telling me to wait. It was very frustrating. I was both anxious and excited about this mission.

In early 2001, I performed at one of Chet Snow's Crystal Skull Conferences with Ani Williams, harpist, Peter Sterling, harpist and gongs, John Dumas, didgeridoo and I, on hand drums. Three major ancient crystals skulls were there, MAX, Synergy, and Mitchell Hedge's skull from Belize. Before our performance, they placed the three skulls on a table in front of the stage lit by colored lights and a strobe light underneath.

Ani asked me to turn off the lights since I was the closest to the light switch. When the main lights were off, all you could see was the crystal skulls light show. The energy was intense. All of us were also sound healers, and we played an abstract piece of spontaneous music. In the middle of the song, I started to leave my body, but I was still playing my hand drum. I was in two worlds at the same time. We could not see the audience. The song went on for 10 minutes. When we finished, Ani asked me to turn the lights back on. At that moment I could not feel the ground, I was still in an altered state. I moved slowly and carefully down the stairs to the light switch. When I turned it on, the whole audience was zoned out with their mouths opened in a frozen position. They looked like statues. We proceeded to play our next song. It took the audience a few more minutes to come out of their altered state.

This is what the ancient Mayan and Egyptians talked about, color, lights, and sound together. This can transport you into multi—dimensional worlds. Your awareness expands and you can see into different realms. What an incredible experience!

I eventually moved down to the Village of Oak Creek in the south end of Sedona with some musician friends. Every night I would go outside and look up at the stars. I remember watching this one big star for days. I felt it was not a star, but a ship. After a few evenings of watching it, I noticed it would rise up from behind one of the large mountains and go towards the East, then stay in that same spot for an hour and go back down behind the same mountain. I said to myself "that is not correct." I know that all stars move toward the west, and they do not go backwards.

One day I watched it until it disappeared behind the mountain. When it was on top of the mountain, it made a large red flash and then dropped quickly behind the mountain. A small white star to the left of it was also flashing red, but that one stayed in the same spot.

A few evenings later I heard faint air raid sirens. I went outside and looked up on top of the same mountain, and saw several black helicopters going back and forth and a small airplane was flying very low circling the neighborhood. After that situation, I never saw the star again. I said to myself, I knew it was a ship.

After a year, I moved back up to West Sedona and got my own place. I never felt comfortable living in the village as it seemed to have a completely different energy there even though it is part of Sedona. I felt more at home in West Sedona. I had a house-warming party and everyone said, of course you feel good here ThunderBeat. Thunder Mountain is right behind your house. That is great! I said. I didn't know it was called Thunder Mountain before I moved there. I just knew the energy was right.

Sept 11th 2001

I did not have TV in my house nor did I want it. For me, television programs are violent, negative, senseless and downright boring. I felt the same way about TV when I was a child.

One day a girlfriend called me and said, "Have you been watching TV?" I said, "No, I don't have TV."

"So you haven't heard the news about the plane crashing into the twin towers?"

"No.'

"They blew up the Twin Towers in New York City. You need to come over and see this."

I drove over to her house right away. When I got there, everyone was crying. I watched the news on TV and saw a jet flying into the Twin Towers. The first words out of my mouth were "New World Order."

The next day the spirit voice "came in" and said, "Okay, it is time now." I knew exactly what he meant. I said, "You know I have been trying to record the Chakra CD for 4 years now." The Voice said again, "It is time now."

I said Okay to the voice and started recording the Chakra Journey CD adding the specific tones for each chakra. This time it worked. Everything flowed nice and smooth. I now realize why spirit stopped me for all those years. There is a certain time when things are supposed to happen. The CD is for healing and awakening. I released the CD and it became a national best seller in 2002.

The testimonies I received were profound. Emails were coming in from people telling me their stories on how it released their stress, emotional issues, fear, and actual physical pain.

The Chakra Journey CD was helping so many people therefore I decided to develop a personal chakra sound healing session which includes shamanic breath work, visualization of the colors of each chakra, Reiki and tuning forks. These sessions went even deeper into the healing and awakening process.

I also started writing a Chakra Workshop, which included information on sound healing. Sound healing was still very new at that time. I remember reading an Edgar Cayce book when I was very young. He said, "Sound will be the medicine of the future." I say, "The future is now"

Edgar Cayce (March 18, 1877-January 3, 1945) was an American psychic who allegedly possessed the ability to answer questions on subjects such as healing and wars. He also gave a reading about Atlantis while in a hypnotic trance. Cayce founded a nonprofit organization, the Association for Research and Enlightenment. Though Cayce himself was a member of the Disciples of Christ and lived before the emergence of the New Age Movement, some believe he was actually the founder of the movement and influenced its teachings. Christians also question his unorthodox answers on religious matters such as reincarnation and Akashic records. However others accept his abilities as "God-given."

One day my friend Diana who is a social worker called me. She said she was having problems with a teenage group that she was coaching.

She was working in a place for teenagers with drug and alcohol addictions and severe family abuse. She said their attention span was next to zero and they were not listening to her. She asked me about my Chakra Journey CD and wondered if I thought it would help. I said, yes absolutely. I taught her the chakra meditation I developed. I then asked her to let me know how it worked out. There were about fifteen young women in the group.

She called me a week later and said it helped a lot. Although they have calmed down, but were having a hard time visualizing the colors of each chakra. I asked, "None of them could see the colors of the rainbow?" She said no. "I said they are totally blocked."

She then suggested that I create a Chakra DVD. I told her that was a great idea, of course color light, and sound together. I was excited. I was on another mission, and I started working on it right away.

I knew exactly what to do. I worked on the DVD for ten hours a day and six weeks straight. When I finished it, I gave her a copy and asked her for the results from the class. She called me a week later excited and said, "It has calmed the whole class down and now they focus better and can see the colors. It has helped me and the girls tremendously." What a great breakthrough! I said. That is wonderful.

I put the DVD out on the market nationally and found out that it also works for calming colic babies. Mothers would play it at night and the babies would sleep through the whole evening without waking.

The day I finished the Chakra Journey DVD, I heard the "Spirit Voice. This voice sounded different. "he said, "Write the book."

"What book?"

"The Chakra book."

"There are many chakra books out there," I said.

"Not like yours. Besides, it will complete your package," he said.

"That does not sound very spiritual," I said.

He did not say anything after that.

I said, okay, now where do I start? I just wrote a Chakra Workshop so I will begin there and use that information.

While writing the book, I heard the Spirit Voice say a few times, "remember the children, remember the children." I was getting very intense with some knowledge so, I rearranged the book and put more fun information in. I also channeled new information about the planets and animal totems for each chakra. Six months later the book was finished.

As soon as I got it back from the printers, I realized it completed my package. Spirit was right! Now my package has the Chakra book, CD, DVD and Chakra poster. Nice!

I am so grateful for my spirit guides.

Later I found out this voice was Thoth that told me to write the Chakra Book and the spirit voice that has been guiding me with my chakra project was Archangel Gabriel. I found this out during my 22-strand DNA activation session in 2005.

After my book release, I received an e-mail from a twelve-year old girl who said she bought the book, read the whole thing and loved it. She was on her way to summer camp so she wanted to know how to keep the amethyst crystal from falling from the crown chakra because she was giving a chakra healing on her father. I said this is incredible. The children are healing the parents. I was so happy when I received her e-mail. This one occurrence made it all worth writing the book.

My next CD project was my Mayan Landing 2012 CD. I had the songs I recorded when I got back from the Mayan lands in 1998. I added the galactic activation tones that I ethereally heard at the Mayan temples. For the CD artwork, I visualized a starship over a Mayan temple beaming a light upon it, to activate the pyramid.

I remember a while back meeting an artist that did sacred site paintings with UFOs over the pyramids and temples. I had taken his number and told him that I might call him one day to do a CD cover that I had in mind. His artwork was perfect. I called his number, but it was disconnected. I asked about him around Sedona and someone told me he moved out of town. No one seemed to know where he went.

In 2003, I was asked to perform at Chet Snow's Crop Circle Conference. I was setting up my table, and low and behold, the artist I was looking for to do my Mayan CD cover was setting up right next to me. I said to him "I can't believe it! I have been looking for you for months, and now here you are right next to me". We talked about the CD cover and he completed the artwork within a week. How magical.

I believe this is divine synchronicity!

Dolores Cannon was speaking at the conference. She was talking about her new book at that time, called "The Custodians: Beyond Abduction." It was about peoples' experiences with alien abductions. That was when I knew I needed a session with her. I asked her if she had time while she was there. She said no, that she was booked up for the next six months. It took me almost a year to get a session with her.

One day I was over at Aluna Joy's house. She was helping me with the final touches of the Mayan CD. I picked her because I liked her artwork and she had been doing sacred tours to the Mayan Lands for many years. Therefore, I knew she was spiritually connected.

When I left her house that sunny clear day, I stopped at the end of her street and looked up at the sky. I saw a small cloud and immediately, I knew it was not a cloud. There were no other clouds in the sky. I watched it for a few minutes and suddenly it disappeared. I kept watching the same spot and sure enough, I saw a small white ship appear. It hovered there for a moment then I watched it adjusting itself. It got longer then it got shorter. It did this a few times and then it started to move slowly across the sky. I watched the oblong-shaped ship until it disappeared.

In 2004, I released my Mayan landing CD. I scheduled a tour to Florida to do some performances and my Chakra Workshops. While there, a shaman contacted me and said he had something for me. I didn't know him. He said Spirit told him to connect with me. We got together for lunch and he gifted me a Condor feather. Wow!!! What an honor! Thank you, Great Spirit!

When I was 16 years old, I received my first feather. It was an Eagle feather. When someone is gifted an Eagle feather, it is considered a high honor.

"Meaning of Feathers:

Feathers mean a lot to Native American Tribes. A feather isn't just something that falls out of a bird, it means much more. The feather symbolizes trust, honor, strength, wisdom, power, freedom and much more. To be given one of these is to be hand picked out of the tribe—it's like getting a gift from a high official.

If any Native American is given an Eagle feather it is one of the most rewarding items they can ever be handed. The Eagle is considered as the most sacred of all birds. For it is the only one that flies the highest to become the messenger for the Creator, and transforms into the angel of love and peace to accept our prayers. The eagle teaches us about our inner strength, offering acts of courage; honor oneself, and others, also how you must walk your own path to seek your vision in life. The eagle's eyes teaches us to see more clearly, so that others do not stump our path, for the Creator offers all of us a journey of peace and love that we must learn. Our life is never perfect, only in spirit we are perfect. So we learn by our mistakes to become a better person, becoming a human being."

Derrick Whiteskycloud

There is an ancient prophesy when these two feathers come together. It is said, *"When the Condor from the south meets the Eagle from the north a new day for Earth will awaken and peace will prevail on Earth".*

At the end of my tour in Florida, on my way back to Arizona, I had scheduled a session with Dolores Cannon. I stopped in at her home in Arkansas. It was a two-and-a-half hour session and there was only time for two of my ET encounters. I know that I had many more. (*This was the same session I found out about what had happened to my mother and me when I was four years old and we were taken up into a spaceship.*)

Dolores brought me back to the situation in Gulf Breeze where I could see what really happened. When I was driving to Jim's house the road and scenery was repeating itself. The best way I can describe it is, that I was in a hologram. I remember the road curved and repeated itself several time. During the session, I saw myself get out of the car, but there was no ground to step on. I got back into my car and now I realize that I was driving on nothing. The orange balls of light that I thought were street lights were continuously circling around my car. When I thought I was inside the bar, instead I was in a room in a spaceship. They laid me down in what seemed to be, a black lounge chair. There was a blue being about seven feet tall standing next to me. It looked like a male and he appeared to be elderly. He was a doctor. He had five fingers and a thumb, his thumb was as long as his fingers. The best way I can describe him is that he looked like a praying mantis.

The people sitting at the horseshoe-shaped bar now to my left were observing what he was doing to me. They all looked like different species. He hooked up what seemed to be six tubes and placed three on the right side of my chest and three on my left. There was a bright, glaring light above me so it was hard to see everything he was doing. I felt that he was doing a healing on my heart and lungs, as I had been a smoker for many years.

Then the ET put his hand inside my stomach. I did not feel anything so there was no pain. Then I saw this round, colorful ball light up and float above me. I watched it go inside of my stomach. I never felt any pain or pressure of any kind, and I have no idea what the purpose for either one of those procedures was. He was very gentle with me so I did not have any fear whatsoever.

When Dolores brought me out of the session, I asked her for a piece of paper. I proceeded to draw the ET figure I saw and told her more information. The people at the bar were different races of beings observing a healing on me. The blue being working on me was a doctor. The couple at Jim's house was from the spaceship and yes, they wanted me to live on their ship. Jim was a worker on the ship and he would go back and forth from the ship to Earth. They said I have been on this ship before and that is why Jim was so familiar to me. This is where I originally met him.

During this session, I finally found out what happened during the 3 hours of missing time in Gulf Breeze, Florida on the way to Jim's house.

There is still more information I want to know. Where are these beings from? In addition, what is their purpose? I did feel at peace from them. I did not feel any fear or negativity from them.

Dolores and I had a late lunch together. During lunch, I felt a little spacey. Dolores said that I might be tired afterwards. It was about 4:00 p.m. and I still had a long drive ahead of me. Her home was in the middle of nowhere and it was a fifty-mile drive to the next town and the interstate route I needed to take.

I then left and started my drive back to Arizona. About thirty miles into the drive, I became extremely tired. It was hard to keep my eyes open. Again, I felt as though I was being followed, but I could not see anyone. When I got to the next town, I was so tired. I knew that I had to get a hotel room right away. My back was beginning to hurt; it felt very sore. I knew I was now feeling the procedure from the ET encounter.

I found a hotel, got into my hotel room and laid down. I immediately started to receive messages. In my 'mind's eye,' I saw a yellow light beaming down on me and a voice said, "Yellow is the color that heals you." Then I saw a purple, three-dimensional pyramid floating above my head, which went into my crown chakra. I remember them calling me "Flying Eagle with Many Wings," and I had just been gifted a condor feather. I saw some other symbols, but now I do not remember. I was so tired I fell asleep. Slowly, the pieces of the puzzle are coming together.

When I got home from my Florida tour, I received a phone call from José Argüelles. He heard my Mayan CD and wanted me to perform at his "Day out of Time" Festival in Ashland, Oregon. He also said there was a three-day conference with James Twyman and Neale Donald Walsch that he was speaking at and wanted me to play a song before he spoke. I was thrilled!

We drove out to Ashland and set up a table with my products at the conference. I brought my friend LionFire and his son with me.

In the afternoon, I performed a song from my Mayan CD. Then José spoke. About a second after he finished, a lightning bolt struck and blew out all the electricity in Ashland. We all went outside and saw a triple rainbow in the sky. Hundreds of people were there and witnessed it. José turned around to me and said, "Thank you ThunderBeat for playing the activation tones." I said, "Thank you. It is an honor to be here and of service."

We became very good friends after that. He invited me down to a ceremony he was doing at Palenque a Mayan temple in Chiapas, Mexico for his birthday. I also said," one day soon I would like you to come to Sedona and speak." He asked me to let him know when and he would be there. In 2006, I produce a conference I called "Earth Changes." I invited Jose to speak and Bear cloud to do his crop circle presentation. Right before Jose spoke, I did a Mayan concert. Over 300 people showed up. That evening at dinner I asked Jose for a testimony on my music for my website He said, "First of all ThunderBeat you are a hard act to follow but I will say your music is the truth and my favorite song is "Galactic Voyage" it reminds me of home." I honor this man greatly he was the one who made the world aware of the Mayan culture back in 1987 with his book the Mayan Factor.

While I was in Palenque, I was leading a chakra ceremony in one of the temples. As soon as I finished, a Mayan elder, deity 'came in' and said in a loud, stern voice, **"We start with the Heart."** I immediately understood what he meant. I asked if anyone else heard the voice and everyone said no. I tuned into him for more information and he proceeded to tell me about the rainbow colors and the ancient order of the chakras for awakening. I thanked him for the information and asked for his permission to do this work. He said yes. I now had a mission from an ancient Maya Elder spirit. I will create a Heart Chakra CD starting with the heart.

A few years went by before I created the "Heart Chakra Journey" CD. I don't know what I was waiting for because I usually move very quickly on missions I receive. I did want a special drum to play the heartbeat on the CD. All the drums I had, I felt were not right.

One day my friend LionFire from the Four Corners area called. He was donating his sacred Powwow drum to the 13 Indigenous Grandmothers for a four-day drum prayer for Mother Earth in Sedona. He asked if he could stay with me while he was here. I told him, of course he could.

After the ceremony on the fifth day, he brought the drum back to my house. This is when I realized that this is the drum I have been waiting for to do the Heart Chakra CD. I asked LionFire if I could record with his drum and he said yes. With all those beautiful prayers and energy in the drum, I felt blessed. It was a divine moment.

The Mayan elder showed me the ancient order of clearing and activating the chakras. Here is the information that came through for the "Heart Chakra Journey" CD.

Heart Chakra
Solar Plexus Chakra
Sacral Chakra
Root Chakra
Heart Chakra
Throat Chakra
Third Eye Chakra
Crown Chakra

Florida Tour 2005

In February 2005, I booked another tour to Florida to teach my Chakra workshop and do some music performances.

Then I received an e-mail telling me that I was nominated for five Native American music awards and that I was to go to the Awards Show. The last time, the Awards Show was in New Mexico. I looked at the date and saw that it was the same time as my tour in Florida. I said Oh No.

When I looked up at where the show was I could not believe my eyes. It was in Florida, and it fit perfectly into my schedule. I was so excited and grateful. Another divine synchronicity!

I ended up receiving two awards for my Mayan Landing 2012 CD, one for Best New Age Recording and the other for Best World Music Recording. I got to see some old friends, and several people wanted healing sessions. What a wonderful blessing.

The last place on my tour was in Gainesville, Florida. I stayed with my friend Amy who was a professional photographer. At the end of my workshop and performance, she wanted to ride back to Arizona with me and then fly back to Florida in a few days. She said she had never been out west. I said Great! I will take you on a tour of the west. I know some incredible sacred sites, and you can stay with me in Sedona." The drive from Florida to Sedona takes three days.

On the drive back home, I noticed a large star following us for two days. I saw it moving and I felt it was watching us. I kept mentioning it to Amy. I pointed it out to her on the second evening at the hotel where we stayed, but she said it just looked like a big star to her.

The third evening we were on to I-17 South from Flagstaff, Arizona to Sedona. I knew this area very well and was familiar with all the exits.

Sedona is only forty minutes away. Amy was driving at that point. It was a beautiful, clear night. I had my window open and I could see the stars everywhere.

I noticed the large star behind us again. We were talking, when all of a sudden I saw the signs for the exits starting to repeat.

I looked out the window and up at the stars again, and the whole sky was all black. Just a minute ago, I had seen hundreds of stars. We passed many exits that I knew never existed. I kept telling Amy," that exit does not exist," and even those exits started to repeat themselves. The energy was similar to the hologram experience that I had in Gulf Breeze.

I said to Amy, "Don't be afraid, but I think we are in a hologram because the exits are repeating themselves." I kept an eye on the clock to see if we would have any time missing. About 20 minutes later, the stars came out and the exits were back to normal. It took us about an hour and half instead of 45 minutes to get to the Sedona Exit. I know something happened but I am not sure what.

I took Amy to see many of the sacred sites in Arizona. She ended up loving it. She said the beautiful sunsets and mountains were a photographer's dream.

22 STRAND DNA ACTIVATION

Later that year my friend Carolyn, from the Galactic Federation Academy of Light, wanted to come to Sedona to do a 22-DNA Activation talk. She said if I held the class at my house, she would give me the 22-DNA Activation session as a trade. I absolutely said yes!

The 22 DNA *activation is a physically administered activation that opens pathways between the physical, crystalline and etheric bodies, allowing new patterns of light to be replicated into the cells of the physical body.*

Your DNA is sacred, personal and unique. It contains codes that determine your body type, behavior patterns, potential diseases and more. Also encoded there is information about your spiritual family, where you came from and why you are here on Earth.

The 22 DNA Activation activates your personal codes for you to help you remember who you are. It activates dormant brain functions to their highest energy potential and original divine function, especially your pineal and pituitary glands.

You will begin to manifest your dormant higher senses like telepathy, clairvoyance, and intuition.

Your DNA holds your family karma. It is passed down from your ancestors and you then pass it on to those who come after you. The activation changes the genetic structure and goes back three to five generations, and ahead three to five generations. It offers the opportunity to clear many things and affects both the past and the future.

The Following Was Transmitted By Archangel Metatron.

CAN I ACTIVATE MY OWN DNA?

(Metatron) "Many technologies are available that will open the DNA up to the 12th strand. Activating strands beyond that requires the services of one who is so trained and initiated at the physical level, one who carries the spiritual authority to do this work.

WHAT ARE THE BENEFITS OF THE 22 DNA STRAND?

Empowers you to maximize your potential to bring forth talents and abilities not yet realized.

Enables you to have more energy and clarity.

Allows releasing of unconscious knowledge stored within.

Creates a greater opening for connecting to the Higher Self. Allows clearing of family and genetic karmic patterns.

Strengthens the immune system and quicker rejuvenation of various organs, tissues and muscles.

It activates dormant brain functions to their original divine function.

It raises your frequency level by bringing more light into the physical body.

You will begin to manifest your higher senses like intuition, telepathy, and clairvoyance.

You only need this activation once in a lifetime, never having to do it again under any circumstance.

Mental Telepathy

I had the 22 DNA Activation from Carolyn. She is a very powerful woman, who channels the Archangels and The Great White Brotherhood of Light, which are supernatural beings of great power who spread spiritual teachings through selected humans. The members of the Brotherhood of light may be known as the Masters of the Ancient Wisdom or Ascended Masters. Carolyn is an ordained minister in the Order of Melchizedek, and serves humanity through the Orders of Maitreya, Melchizedek, Quan Yin, the Ashtar Command, and the Council of 36.

Amazing things happened during the activation. Carolyn said to tell her what I was experiencing. Here is a short outline of what I experienced.

What I saw first were many colors of red, white, and black. She said those are the Atlantean colors. Then the color indigo came in, followed by a choir of voices.

I saw babies with wings circling my head. She said those are cherub angels. I looked into the eyes of the baby angels and they were not like babies. I could see and feel that they were highly intelligent beings. Then I saw colors of blue and purple and heard a voice saying, "This is Archangel Gabriel and I have been working with you for years, and you do not even recognize me."

Carolyn did not hear the voice. I asked her if Archangels have egos and she started to laugh. She said no, but they do like to be recognized. I said that is exactly what Archangel Gabriel just said to me.

Then I heard him say, "You can clear darkness just by toning with your voice." I then heard the sound of trumpets. The colors of gold and white came in. I saw myself walking on an island of clouds and saw myself with white wings with touches of pink.

She then brought me back to Earth and said you will always be in touch with this place while you are here. She said now the light in your body will increase over the years. I was so at peace and yet greatly energized. Now I know that one of the voices I hear is Archangel Gabriel. He is the Angel that was helping me with my Chakra Journey CD. He knew the perfect time to release it for healing the people on the planet. *Thank you Archangel Gabriel, Much Gratitude.*

Gabriel is known as the messenger of God and the bringer of good news and hope. This Archangel was said to have appeared to Mary to give her news of the birth of Jesus. Gabriel brings news of one's spiritual destiny that the soul has agreed to do in this lifetime. Gabriel also teaches us that no destiny is more important than another's is. Gabriel holds the books of knowledge. He was with Spirit at the beginning of creation and noted in his records the destiny and focus of each individual Soul as it came into being. This makes this Archangel of extreme importance in understanding one's path through life and its overall greater significance. Gabriel is said to appear to them who are ready to grasp and move forward on their destiny, and in so doing Gabriel brings an ever-increasing abundance of messages and hope that what one is seeking may be manifested or accomplished. Gabriel speaks too many.

Part of the "job" of this Archangel is to make us more aware that we are always receiving messages from the Universe. They are all around us and yet so often we walk right past the signs and omens that are designed to answer our every question, or the signs that point the way to our greatest success and fulfillment. Gabriel is also the bringer of resurrection and the knowledge that nothing ever dies but simply changes to a different form and is born anew in other realms of existence.

In 2012, I had a strong sensation that I was supposed to learn how to do the 22-DNA Activation for people. I asked Carolyn if she would teach me. She said only certain people are allowed to receive this training and it was only available to initiated members of the ancient mystery schools like priests, priestesses, oracles and leaders like kings and pharaohs.

I told her I have a strong sense of knowing that I am supposed to do this work.

She said that she would have to ask The Great White Brotherhood of Light if I was allowed to be initiated, and trained for this work. She called me the next day and said, "Yes, they said you have the rites and you are actually destined to do this work".

In 2012, I had my initiation and training to do the 22-Strand DNA Activation sessions, which brings the 22 Keys of Light into the body. This is the next step for humanity's ascension. What a wonderful opportunity to help people come into the higher dimension of light.

While writing this book, I was thinking about the numbers 202-20-30 that came to me back in Florida. I said to myself, "I have not read those numbers from the Keys of Enoch since 1998. I looked up the numbers again, and to my amazement; it references the 22 Keys of Light activation and the 22 strands of DNA. This is why the Voice said to me many years ago "Your number is 202-20-30." I was so excited. Now I fully understand. This is part of the work I chose to do while I am here on Earth. Another wonderful piece of the puzzle is put together.

Carolyn kept talking about getting a soul portrait done by a woman here in Sedona named Celeste. She said she was brilliant and has been channeling messages and drawing soul portraits for numerous years. I have seen her Angel paintings around Sedona. I made an appointment for a soul portrait reading with Celeste.

During the session, she called in her spirit guides and angels for information. She also recorded the session while painting the soul portrait. At the beginning of the reading, she shouted, "How am I going to put all that on one piece of paper?"

I thought she was yelling at me. She said, "No, I am talking with my guides."

As she continued to draw she said, "You have been to so many star systems that I had to figure out how to put them all down on one piece of paper.

She said, "You were a Commander of your own ship and you came down to Ancient Egypt to teach the people about the universal knowledge and the creation story of the Gods and Goddesses. You became very upset with the people because they were not listening to the knowledge that you were conveying. The reason was they were in awe of you and honored you as a God. All you wanted to do was help them advance. Therefore, you ended up writing it down for them."

She said, "This became part of the Ancient Egyptian mystery school. This time you volunteered to incarnate to help in the ascension process for the people and the planet by means of color, light and sound. She said I brought in the pink and green rays for them." Pink is unconditional love and green is healing. She said, "You work with Thoth the Atlantean and you have a major heart connection together".

She continued to say, "The Lions are my protectors because I saved them when one of their planets from the Lyra Constellation was destroyed in a Draconian war. I brought them to Sirius and gave them a new place to live."

This is why people think the Lion race is from Sirius, but they are from the Lyra Constellation.

She then proceeded to say that I was on the Ashtar ship when they brought Jesus down to Earth, and the Bethlehem star was the Ashtar ship. She said my number is seven on the council of twelve with the white brotherhood and we all were preparing Him for Earth.

Now I understand why I was so upset when I first heard that Jesus died on the cross, and I do remember telling Him that he had to repeat Himself because it takes people on Earth a long time to understand things. In addition, I knew the paintings at the ancient tombs and temples in Egypt were ancient knowledge from the stars, not just the stories of the pharaohs' or queens, as the Egyptologist's Claim. More of the wonderful pieces of the puzzle have come together for me.

This reading was incredible. I received a tremendous amount of information to process. At that time, I had heard of Ashtar Command, but I wanted to know more about them.

Celeste is amazing! She received so much detail. She even drew a space ship on the portrait while conveying all the information. She has such a BIG heart.

I honor her and highly recommend a soul portrait reading from her.

Celeste's Website: http://www.artsedona.net/index.html

EAGLE AND THE CONDOR CEREMONY

Adam Yellowbird invited me to the first known "Eagle and the Condor Ceremony" in the United States with the Hopi.

I met Adam Yellowbird in 2003. He lives in the surrounding area of Sedona. Adam is a visionary and spiritual leader, and is the founder of the Global Earth Dance Gathering and The Institute for Cultural Awareness. His vision of "Earth Dance 8" has brought thousands of people together of all color, race, and spiritual background to celebrate and dance around the world. Adam also helps people explore the inner healing of the heart, dreams, and spirit. He is bringing the multi-cultural vision of all people coming together as one for unity and the healing of Mother Earth. He believes we are the Earth Keepers of our Mother and we must take care of her as she takes care of us, the people.

Adam is asking all people to wake up and listen to their heart, the Holy Spirit, and bring out what has been hidden away for eons within one's being. Remember, we are all divinely moved by the Holy Spirit to do what is in the highest good for all humanity. Today, take your steps forward!

According to Yellowbird, the Eagle and the Condor Ceremony holds a unique opportunity for humanity to listen to Mother Earth, heal emotions and the sacred Feminine through the element of water, bring all the elements back into balance, re-member our connection to the natural world, and break through barriers with cultural exchange.

"We can all be sparks on the front line, giving the New Civilization a foundation. We can become illuminated beings," explains Yellowbird. The Gathering provides us with an "opportunity to come back together, to really go inward and project ourselves into the next place."

The process begins with purification, says Yellowbird: vision quest, fasting, sweat lodges, taking care of the Earth, changing our diet, respecting our fellow relations by purifying disagreements and arguments through communication. All this allows us to be more open to hearing the Earth and less caught up in the mind games of separation.

"We have a chance to re-member ourselves, bring our pieces back together," he says. "Old ways and experiences may block the new information. We must vision goals and dreams of reuniting rather than being stuck in old paradigms. We have to decide where we want to look. We must reprogram our minds. Our nature is to look at the negative. We must look into our hearts and share the dream of making a difference."

Adam Yellowbird brings indigenous elders from South America to the USA to speak of the Ancient knowledge and truth fulfilling many indigenous prophecies from around the world.

In 2007, Adam Yellowbird asked the Native American Hopi to come to Sedona to do the Eagle and the Condor Ceremony while the indigenous tribes from South America were in town. The Mayans, Peruvians and the tribes from South America are the Condor from the South.

The Hopi represent the Eagle from the North. The word, "Hopi" means peaceful ones. Their villages spread out across the northern part of

Arizona and have always viewed their land as sacred. They have never taken the Eagle dance off their reservation before, but they agreed it was time to bring the Eagle from the North together with the Condor from the South for peace to prevail on Earth.

The Mayan prophecies predicted that upon this meeting, two ceremonies would be performed. The first would celebrate the final 13-year cycle of the Mayan calendar. The second ceremony would be of the eagle and the condor—for the indigenous and non-indigenous peoples of the world. The Mayan Prophecies say this meeting will eventually lead to world peace.

The ceremony was held in a lower canyon in Sedona. It was by invitation only. I felt extremely honored and grateful to be invited.

The Hopi said this is where the Star Kachinas first came in. One of the Hopi Elders showed me the area and said there is a major portal there. (Another word for Vortex)

The South Americans did the Condor dance and then the Hopi did their Eagle dance. This was the first ceremony. The second was when they both danced together. It was a beautiful, peaceful ceremony.

As I looked up at the sky, I saw two large clouds shaped exactly like birds right above where the ceremony was taking place. I remember my friend JC teaching me about the cloud beings and yes, they were there. It was magical and an honor to witness this incredible moment.

In 2007, I was invited to perform a concert at the UFO Skywatch Conference in Sedona. The conference was fabulous, and there was great new information that I had never heard before. "Ed Grimsley, the producer of the conference, invited me out to a private UFO sky watch with his military grade, night vision goggles. I could see all kinds of moving objects as I looked at the night sky through these goggles. Ed pointed out objects with his laser light pen that would go back and forth, circle around and then stop and stay in one position for a long period of time. We also saw several objects in pairs moving across the sky. None of this you can see with the naked eye.

In a one-hour period, we saw 48 UFO'S in the sky. It was amazing. They were definitely not airplanes because they moved extremely fast and did unbelievable maneuvers. In addition, he said they are too high up and too many of them to be helicopters.

I then told him some of my ET experiences. I asked him, "Who is the Mystery speaker that you advertised in the brochure?" He said well . . . I would like you to be the Mystery speaker at the conference. At that time, I had only told friends some of my ET experiences and encounters, but never to a large audience. This would be a perfect situation to share my ET stories.

After my talk, people came up to me, and shared their ET stories and said they had similar experiences. Many said they had no one they could to talk to about them and that they felt very comfortable and relieved to be able to tell me their story. I understood because I had experienced the same thing. It makes me feel so good when I can help people.

In 2008, I returned to Egypt for the second time. One temple that was not open when I was there in 1997 was the Temple of Osiris in Abydos. It is one of the oldest temples in Egypt. This is where the Flower of Life symbol is and not found in any other temple in Egypt.

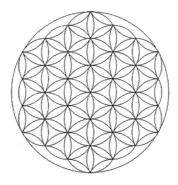

Flower of Life Symbol

The Abydos flower of life examples from Egypt are worthy of note. Claims that they are over 6,000 years old and may date back to as long ago as 10,500 BC or earlier have not yet been confirmed. It was originally thought that the Temple of Osiris in Abydos, Egypt contained the oldest known examples of the Flower of Life. It is now known that an earlier example of the pattern can be seen in the Assyrian rooms of the Louvre Museum in Paris. the Flower of Life and the Seed of Life are linked with the Biblical prophet Enoch, the Archangel Metatron, the six days of Creation, the Vesica Pisces religious symbol, and Borromean rings.

At Abydos temple, when I looked at the walls of hieroglyphs and pictures, I recognized and understood the stories they were conveying. It was the Ancient Egyptian creation story. This was the first place where I could decipher the stories out of all the temples I have been too. This temple seems and feels more familiar to me than the other ones.

The Egyptologist pointed at one of the pictures towards the ceiling. It showed four different kinds of crafts. I lost my breath because one of the ships that Celeste had drawn on my soul portrait painting was there. It is the middle one on the right of the picture.

Osiris Temple in Abydos, Egypt photo by Devara ThunderBeat

When I got back from Egypt, I started composing an Egyptian CD. I wanted to hear some authentic ancient Egyptian melodies. Channeling became much easier for me at this point. Through asking with an open heart, you can receive any information you desire. Therefore, I called in RA, the Sun God and asked him for ancient Egyptian music. After the third day of asking, he started waking me up at 1:00 a.m. and I would hear beautiful ancient Egyptian melody lines.

My recording studio is in my house, so I would get up and record what I heard right away. I wrote a RA song in honor of him, and I remembered the Hathor song I heard at the Karnack temple in Egypt in 1997. I placed those angelic voices in the RA song as well.

In 2010, I completed ten songs and sent the CD to radio stations around the world. It hit Number 1 at many stations and received a ZMR music award nomination for best chill/groove CD of the year. The voters are music directors from radio stations all over the world. It stayed on the top 100 World Music Charts for eight months.

Thank you, Sun God Ra!

One evening that summer (2010) I was outside in my backyard. It was about 1:00 a.m. I had been peacefully meditating for only a few minutes when I saw a red star object moving towards me. It got very big and then turned white. It hovered above me for about five minutes, then like a beacon of light, it got bright and then dark, and then bright again. I felt its presence strongly.

Information started to come from the star. It said, "We are from the Red Star called Nibiru and we bring messages of peace. We are here to make sure the humans are advancing their levels of consciousness. Negative things have been said about us by the ones in fear. We only want good things for this planet and the humans that reside here. Our home planet will be here in your year of 2012. We will be traveling behind your sun. At that time, it will seem as though there are two suns. Your sun will be protecting you from our strong magnetic pull. As of one passing long ago we were here, we traveled in front of your sun and our magnetic energy pulled on the Earth's tectonic plates that caused earthquakes on the land you called Atlantis.

The next thing I remember I woke up in my bed. I looked at the clock and it was 6:00 a.m. I do not remember going into my house and lying down at all, but I do remember the message. They also told me they were the scout ships that come to Earth and check on things before Nibiru comes into our area. Nibiru was the closest to Earth on June 21, 2012. Many people said they saw two suns before, during, and after that time in 2012.

In 2010, I decided to write a theatrical show called, "Egyptian Sun Gods and Goddesses." It is the knowledge of the Ancient Egyptian Creation story. The messages from this story are profound and with color, light, and sound activation. This show will teach and awaken many to some incredible hidden truths. I call it, "Edutainment."

I was not sure who to present this show to since it was a large production and needed to get financial support. I called the entertainment director from the Luxor (Pyramid Resort in Las Vegas) and asked if he would be interested in seeing my presentation. He said, "Yes!"

I went to Las Vegas with a friend of mine and rented a room at the Luxor for a few days. I showed him the video and the storyline. He fell in love with it. He said it would be perfect for the Luxor (The Luxor in Las Vegas is a huge pyramid with an Egyptian theme) then he asked me who my investors were. I said I do not have any. He said we do not invest in any shows. Call me when you find investors. I was very disappointed. This is where the show stands now.

That evening I was in my room at the Luxor on the 22nd floor. I was looking out the window and saw only one star. I watched it for a while. Then a plane came by and what I thought was a plane, stopped at the star for a few minutes. It slowly took off and the star was gone. I said to myself, well that was not a plane or a star. Planes cannot hover and stars do not disappear. I told my friend Élan, who came with me to Vegas and she asked, "Why do you always see UFO's?" I said, "You have to watch the stars for long periods of time, which I do. Most people just glance at them for a moment.

LOOK UP!

In 2011, the Egyptian soundtrack won a Phoenix Producers Choice Award, and in 2012, won an L.A. Music Award for best theatrical sound track. Woo woo!!! I am very excited about putting on this show. One day soon, I hope.

THE 13 CRYSTAL SKULL LEGEND

In ancient times, the crystal skulls were kept inside a pyramid in a circle that created tremendous power known as the Ark. The Ark was comprised of the twelve skulls from each of the sacred planets with the thirteenth skull in the middle, the largest, placed in the center of this formation. This thirteenth skull represents the collective consciousness of all the worlds. Similar to a living library, each skull is like one volume in a set of encyclopedias.

CRYSTAL SKULL CEREMONY 11:11:11

In November 2011, I went to Los Angeles with LionFire for the 11:11:11 Crystal Skull Conference. It was about a ten-hour drive. When we got there, it was sold out.

I said, "We just came thousands of miles, now what?"

As soon as I said that, a man came up to LionFire and said, "The Elders are doing a ceremony out on the land in 40 minutes and both of you are invited. We will caravan there all together." LionFire and I both looked at each other and said at the same time, "This is why we are here, for the Crystal Skull 11:11:11 Ceremony, not the conference."

We had lunch at the hotel dining area where the conference was being held. A woman came over to our table from the conference and we invited her to join us. She told us her story. She had been working in the corporate world all her life. She said that in the past she would make fun of conferences like this and the New Age community.

"One day I woke up and knew that I was supposed to be a healer," she said.

She did not know anything about healing so she had taken some healing courses just a few months before. As soon as she finished, she realized how corrupt the corporate world was so she quit her job and is now doing healings full time. We both told her we have been seeing people shift quickly into the new world and many are becoming healers. We both congratulated her and told her to keep up the good work.

LionFire and I then proceeded to the ceremony. About twenty of us went together to a large mountaintop called Monks Mound in Los Angeles. Mayan Elder Hunbatz Men, a Tibetan Elder, and two Lakota Elders were leading the ceremony. Several people brought their crystal skulls and placed them in the circle of the ceremony. Hunbatz

Men began. It started to rain lightly. Hunbatz Men put his finger up and said, "Not now!" The rain stopped.

During the ceremony, large rays of color came through the clouds from the east. It looked like a rainbow, but the colors were green, pink, and yellow. Green is for healing the heart; pink is unconditional love, and yellow is the Christ light energy. The sun was in the west so the colors were not from the sun. I said, LionFire look at the beautiful healing rays of color in the sky. LionFire saw them too, and took a picture, but they did not come out on the photograph.

It was a lovely ceremony. I felt that the colorful rays in the sky bestowed a healing on Los Angeles.

In December 2011, while praying to Great Spirit, God, I said, "I am so tired of the doom and gloom and lies about the 2012 prophecy. It is creating so much fear. This needs to stop! What can be done about this?"

Thunder Voice "came in" and said, "You know the truth. You speak about this to several now."

The Voice gave me courage. I wrote down all the things that needed to be addressed and ten pages of information flowed through my fingertips.

In the spring of 2012, I spoke at Unity of Sedona about the Mayan Prophesies and the Earth changes. I said, "We should be celebrating this time. We are coming out of the darkness and into the light. The Earth will not shift her axis. She is raising her frequency, as all things are, you, me, the plants and animals. We are all shifting to a higher vibration of light together."

Grandfather Martin, an Elder from the Hopi tribe was there, and said, "You are speaking the truth," and gave me his blessings. I felt highly honored.

In late spring, I spoke at another conference in Sedona. Again, Grandfather Martin showed up and gave me a Corn Blessing. After my talk, I performed a Mayan concert with color visuals to help activate everyone into a higher light. I could feel the Love fill the room. Many thanked me for all the positive knowledge and music and said they felt their fears released. Yeah!!!

Chapter 4

THE CONNECTION

Jesus and Mary Appear

In the fall of 2012, I scheduled a Mayan prophesies talk and healing tour to New Hampshire and Boston. The healings were with my Chakra DVD along with a guided Color—Light Sound meditation. In New Hampshire, 30 women showed up for my presentation. After the talk, I started the Chakra DVD, which goes through the symbols and the colors for each chakra.

Right after the Throat Chakra activation, Jesus came in on the large screen; He was moving and looking at me. Then Mary appeared on the screen. She was wearing a shroud and her eyes were full of love. She looked at me and raised her hands up into a prayer position. Then the screen faded into the symbol of the Third Eye chakra.

Suddenly, rainbow fractals "came in" and started spinning on the screen. This is not on my DVD. I looked down at the left side of the screen, and it said "No disc in computer." I knew this was a divine intervention. I did not want to interrupt anything, so I watched it without saying a word. After about five minutes, I felt that it was ending and that is when I told the group that the fractals were not on my DVD. Everyone looked at the screen and saw the fractals. The DVD ended, and no one knew what to say. The owner of the projector asked me if I had taken the DVD out of the projector. I said that I hadn't. "Well, it says there is no DVD in the projector." She opened up the DVD player and my DVD was there. She said she never saw that before.

It was amazing!!! Everyone was in a blissful state. Jesus and Mary appeared on Earth. We were all blessed that day on 9-9-12. Thank you, Jesus and Mary.

Fractal

My next speaking and healing engagement was in Salem, Massachusetts. One of the women from New Hampshire brought a friend to my talk. She told me she was very touched by the last healing and that her friend needs some healing. I finished my talk and started the chakra DVD. This time, the Chakra DVD played normally all the way through. When it got to the Third Eye chakra, the woman who saw it before dropped her mouth open in amazement. We both smiled at each other as I nodded my head at her. After the chakra healing activation, her friend came up to me and thanked me. She said she felt so much better.

12:12:12 STAR KNOWLEDGE CONFERENCE, PHOENIX, AZ

The founder of the Star Knowledge Conference is Golden Eagle, aka Standing Elk. The first conference was held in Estes Park, Colorado in 1996. The one I attended. There have been many more since then.

12:12:12 Star Knowledge Conference was a five-day conference not to be missed. My friends from Los Angeles, Angelica and Evan, from their Soul Shrine Band asked me to perform with them at the conference. I also got a solo spot to perform, do some healing work, and got a table to sell my healing products.

For five days there were powerful ceremonies going on for the people and the planet. The energy was incredible. I had the opportunity to catch up with so many friends that I had not seen in years. Hunbatz Men came to my table. After all these years of knowing him, he finally saw my Mayan Landing CD with the spaceship on it activating a Mayan temple. He pointed to the CD and announced to all his family members. "That is it! This is what is happening". He held up the CD to show them. I told him I saw that as prophesy for 2012 in 1998. "That is when I first met you." He listened to the CD and loved it. I gifted him a CD and a Mayan poster, and he was extremely grateful. By that first afternoon, I was sold out of all my products.

That evening Grammy winner Yolanda Martinez was performing right before Soul Shrine. I have known her for many years. She asked me to perform with her. It was so much fun and we received a standing ovation. The next day when we talked, we both said at the same time, "Let's do a CD together!" I said, "What will we call it?" She said "Thunder Beings," of course, because we are both Thunder Beings."

Here is a Native American legend about Thunder Beings:

It is the arrival of the thunderbeings who bring the final transformation. The thundercloud full of purifying rain, the lightning that shatters false reality. Only your true identity will live through the cleansing of the thunderbeings, for you will be reborn in the heart of All That Is.

Many of the people that came to the conference received miraculous healings and awakenings. The future to me looks very bright!

UFO CONFERENCE PHOENIX, AZ—FEBRUARY 2013

I set up a table to sell my color—light—sound healing products at the 5-day UFO Conference in Phoenix. My friend Tina came with me. The people who go to these conferences are always very interesting. I never know what is going to happen.

At this conference, I met Travis Walton, the author of "Fire in the Sky."

FIRE IN THE SKY is a 1993 science fiction horror drama film based on an alleged extraterrestrial encounter, directed by Robert Lieberman, and written by Tracy Tormé based on Travis Walton's book *The Walton Experience.*

I told him I have had contact many times and my experiences were positive ones. My main question to him was, "What was the gooey, storage chamber for humans all about?" He said, "That was all made up by Hollywood, and yes, I was in fear when they contacted me because I did not know what was going on. Now, as I reflect back on the experience, it was a good one. I am rewriting a script to being a more positive one."

"That is great news," I said. "I am so glad you are doing that. I am tired of all the doom and gloom, and fear and LIES about ETs."

I then met a female hybrid at the conference. I knew right away because the outline of her facial skin was a bluish color and the middle of her face was pink, not the beige or white that you normally see. She sat down at my table to listen to my music. I wanted to mention to her that I knew she was a hybrid, but she seemed very shy, closed down and guarded. Tina looked at her and said, "Yes, she is definitely a hybrid."

When I saw her the next day, I said to Tina, "I have to say something to her."

I approached her and said, "Do you know that you are a hybrid?" She looked at me, nodded her head, and said "Yes!"

Her friend who was standing beside her said, "I kept saying something to you about that but you never answered me. I knew there was something different about you."

The hybrid woman said to me, "Yes, I could tell you many stories about my mother and me." She was very shy. Then she walked away.

The next people I met were a group of psychic readers and healers. They said they were offering a triple reading with all three of them. One did a healing, one drew a picture at the same time as the healing, and the third person gave you a message at the end. I felt their intentions were pure so I signed up.

The healer sat me down in a chair. Then he held both of my hands, and after a few minutes he looked up at me with a surprised look on his face, and said, "Did you know you came in with the golden light? Do you know what that means?"

"Well, the golden light is Christ consciousness."

"Yes, he said. And, you have wings."

I then told him that I remembered seeing my wings when I was in Egypt. He said, "Most people have angels around them, but you are an angel." I blushed and then smiled.

He went on to say that, I have been carrying heaviness for the planet, and he was going to release it now. I said okay and thanked him.

When he was done, the woman who was drawing the picture for the reading had also finished. She asked me if I was Jewish. I said no, why? She said the Star of David 'came in'.

"Oh, that is my astrology chart. The day I was born the planets were in the position that formed a Star of David, which is probably what you're tuning into."

She then said that when I am sleeping I travel through many portals and I have found a planet where there is water to cleanse myself from the heavy debris of the Earth, and that I turn myself into a mermaid and swim in those waters on that planet.

She also said that I have a Draconian hook in me to slow me down. When I got home, I had a friend check to see if this was true. She said that I did, and removed the hook with her radionics machine.

The woman who did the third message said that I wrote a lot of music in the 10th dimension before I came to Earth and manifested it on Earth. She was talking about my Cosmic Dream CD that has music from different star systems, and my DNA Activation CD, which I just released prior to the UFO conference.

Another interesting booth at the conference was a man checking people for ET implants. It was a 30-minute procedure. Tina and I both signed up.

He found three implants in Tina and he said I had seven. The man also said that I have had contact within the last two days. HMMM, how could that be? I do not remember that and I had been here at the conference for three days.

STARMAN

On the second to last day of the conference, a man arrived at my booth and just stood there staring at the woman who was talking to Tina. I thought he was with her and waiting for her. I asked him if he would like to listen to my music and he said no, and just stood there in front of my table looking at nothing.

A few minutes later, he looked at me and said, "Yes, I will listen to your music." While listening with the headphones, he picked up my chakra book, opened it up and then just stared out into space again. He then put it down, jumped up quickly, started asking me question after question about chakras and my music without giving me any time to answer them.

He then walked away. I thought that was very strange.

I said to the woman talking to Tina "Your friend just left." She said, "I do not know him." I said, "The man was just standing there as if he was waiting for you." She said, "No, I never saw him before."

Now that I think about it, his actions reminded me of the man in the movie "Starman" with Jeff Bridges. All three of us watched him walk around the room and just stand in front of merchandise booths and did the same thing he just stared into space.

The UFO conference was a lot of fun. Dolores Cannon was also speaking there and as usual, she had lots of wonderful new information about the energies of Earth and the Extraterrestrials.

MARCH 16TH 2013

My hypnosis session with Nina Anderson Flagstaff, AZ

I wanted to find out more information about my ET encounters. The session with Delores Cannon covered two situations, and I had numerous encounters when I lived in Florida.

Dolores is so popular now that she is booked up for years. Therefore, I found Nina, a hypnotherapist in Flagstaff, who was trained by Dolores. I made an appointment with her.

The day of the session, when I got to Flagstaff, I saw two cloud ships in the sky and strongly felt their presence.

When I arrived at Nina's house, we talked for a while before the session.

When we started the session, I instantly saw a purple object floating in front of me. It was spinning and seemed to take on a tetrahedron shape. Then the color Indigo 'came in' turning to blue then green. The colors were going down the Chakra system. When it got to the yellow, the solar plexus, I took off and flew up above the clouds. I looked down and saw a male angel with large white wings flying above the clouds and the Earth. He had brown hair. I turned around and I was then face to face with Jesus; he was dressed in a green robe. He opened his arms and we embraced in a beautiful, loving hug. I told this to the therapist and she asked, "What is your relation to Jesus?" I said he is my brother.

Then I was transported into a ship, I was being taken somewhere. I was standing in the front of the ship staring through a window. Two beings were behind me. We started moving very fast through a long white tunnel or portal. We curved to the left then to the right. We came to a star system, I saw a pure white planet, and the sky around it was purple and black. I asked, "Where are we?" "We are in the Sirius Constellation a male voice said, and this is your home, Commander—Doc."

The ship stopped in front of the planet. There was a purple being with a triangle-shaped head with some kind of headdress on and it was circling and scanning me in front of the planet.

I asked, "What is the reason for this?" They said to make sure and remove all immoral implants before entering into the planet. I then heard machine noises and saw a doorway opening to go inside the planet. We proceeded inside through another tunnel. It seemed as though I was in a different craft because there were windows on the sides of this one. We were moving at a slower pace. Along the sides of this tunnel, there was a place where people or beings could walk and large windows along the walkway. I saw many star beings. They were all pink from head to toe peering through the windows inside our craft as we passed by. "They are very curious and excited about seeing you Commander," a voice said. The therapist asked who they were, and I replied, "My family". There are some I have not seen in a long while, and others I have never met. Yet, they heard about me coming and are excited to see me."

I was transported into a round room with a large window or a three dimensional screen of some sort. Again, they called me Commander. Commander, a male voice said, "The light is coming now to Earth that we are sending."

The room then filled with colors, misty colors. They talked about the Earth and told me to turn around. On another screen, they showed me Earth as they see it. The Earth was full of dark, smoky clouds due to pollution and combustion. It looked extremely dark, not the colored planet that we see.

They said, "We have been purifying and cleansing the planet for centuries, Commander." They showed me yellow and green waves of light that they placed around the planet for purifying, and said they were also sending rainbow light.

Then they said, "If we did not do this, Planet Earth would have never survived. It would have turned into a dark, dead planet." They showed me a picture of a black, round piece of coal. They also said the frequencies of the nuclear plants on Earth are not correct. They said they put golden light-shaped domes around the nuclear plants for protection. "We need to know Commander what else is required for Planet Earth." I said, "More LOVE."

I turned to look at the being that was talking to me. He was almost translucent. His eyes were triangular-shaped with golden pupils, and small white feathers for hair.

His name is Salu and he is a Commander, too. Another voice said to me, "Salu is my link post master on Sirius whom I communicate with and send information from Earth. They said we work closely together. He is the left postposition and I am the right."

I said, "Thank you for bringing me here. I can breathe here." They all started laughing, and I laughed with them. As we all laughed together, I saw pure, golden light fill the room. If this is home, I feel so at peace here. It is full of pure love and stunning vibrant colors.

They told me that Planet Earth has much fear, which makes the energy dark. It puts a veil over everyone so people cannot see clearly. Everyone is in fear, not one group, but everyone! It is making the planet sick.

They showed me the energy and the color of fear. It was dense, dark and black. "Sickness is what fear creates," they said. "We are now sending Earth more golden light with green rays making it a lime-green color. They continued to say, "People need to be open in order to receive. It is that easy. It is a living Light. Be open to the Light."

The therapist asked a question, "There are many light workers on the planet who are getting very tired. How can we rejuvenate?"

I said, "Step out of fear and surround yourself with pink and golden light. Colors are frequencies of energy that transform all things. Pink is unconditional love and gold is Christ consciousness. Visualize and surround yourself with these colors as often as you can. This will raise your vibration. Colors are extremely essential."

Then they said, during the shifts from 2005 to 2012, Earth has moved closer to the Sirius Constellation.

"We have been waiting a long time for you to write this book. Thank you for telling the Earth people about us."

They proceeded to tell me that there is a big shift coming soon. "We will be sending white and golden light together to Earth. It is time for major transformation. This is huge, a tremendous awakening will happen with the white and golden light frequencies. Everyone will experience an increase in levels of awareness. Even the governments will awaken to the light. This will shift the planet's energy very quickly. Right now, the Earth's energy is orange, which means it is extremely emotional. Too much emotion is causing Earth to be out of balance, resulting in negativity, anger, drama, jealousy, and wars".

The therapist asked, "Why did you choose to come to this planet at this time?"

I said, "To move things along faster. This planet and people move very slowly. It takes people a long time to learn things and they repeat the same mistakes over and over again."

Therapist: "How do you help to move things along?"

"I can remove fear and raise the vibration through sound, light and color frequencies. For example, using color, light, and sound with my music and visuals I am able to heal hundreds of people at the same time. Color is Sound, Sound is Color. This raises their vibration and awareness. Certain tones will activate and clear the negativity from people's minds and hearts and release the fear. Since our solar system is in a free-will zone, all beings have a choice of which direction they want to go in. You can be of Love and Light or you can be in the dark, dense energies. It is your choice."

They reminded me of my number 202-20-30. This is the information for the work I am now doing to help the people shift and to remember who they are. The 22 DNA activation light codes quickly transform people into the higher light.

"They are now bringing in more beings, ones that know me and I know them. They are beings of golden light and they are very happy to see me. They are so beautiful."

I then asked if my mother was a Sirian. They said yes, and then she appeared to me. She was golden with pink light all around her. She is so beautiful, full of radiant love. She told me the only reason she came to Earth was to bring me in.

I started to cry.

My mother was so sweet and full of love.

I remember when I was young, for many years my mother would often say, "People are so mean here on this planet. Why are they so mean? I want to go home."

My mother is with me all the time they said. I asked about my father and they said he is not here; he is an Orion warrior. This made sense to me because his energy was harsh. I then asked about Sheba ThunderDog, and they said, "She is a Commander, too!"

I laughed and they said, "People do not realize that animals are a big part of the mission and they have a high multi-dimensional awareness. They are extremely intelligent, more than humans can understand at this time."

They said, "We always protect you. Just ask and you shall receive."

I asked about my friend from Australia, Hartmut, who designed the book cover. He is an artist always drawing spaceships. They said, "He is your brother and he comes home to Sirius often."

I asked about the triangle ship that used to follow me. "Who was that?" (Remote controlled by the mother ship) They were checking up on me and sending me information.

I asked the therapist if she had any questions for them. She said that she did.

"A lot of people are experiencing tones in their ears and feeling they might have tinnitus. Do they know what this could be?"

"Yes, it is brother Ashtar who is sending beams of blue light to raise people's frequency, which prepares them for the next shift. Sirius sends golden light. We are working together."

They confirmed that when I was in Gulf Breeze at the 1997 UFO Conference, the man Jim, who looked familiar to me was from the Ashtar ship. They brought me on board and gave me a healing. They were the ones that asked me to live on their island, which was their spaceship. They have many races from all over our galaxy on board the Ashtar ship, beings from the Pleiades, Orion, Arcturus, Sirius and more.

Many beings from many star systems are working together to help the people and our planet Mother Earth. The Reptilians are not all bad. There are good ones, too. Some of them do a lot of Light work. They showed me a vision of male reptile being. He looked human, except his pupils were like cat's eyes. I actually saw golden light around him.

ASHTAR COMMAND, Are universal ambassadors of peace. They are here to assist Planet Earth and its humanity in this cycle of cleansing and realignment. Their main teaching and message is spiritually focused, above anything else they have thousands of representatives on Earth and representatives born on Earth as volunteers, to help the planetary Ascension. They have Commanders and embodied Rays of Light. Commanders act consciously, subconsciously and super consciously. Each vibrational tone connects them with certain archives. They are connected with the Christ heart of the Light. They are based on Earth to facilitate the earthly humanity to the fifth dimension. They serve as participants in the birth of humanity from the physical density to the light bodies physical/etheric, capable of ascending to the fifth dimension with the Earth.

They said, we need to raise the frequency but we have to do this slowly. Otherwise, your physical bodies would not be able to handle the change.

I asked them what the colorful ball of light was that they put inside my belly when I was on the Ashtar ship. They said it was a frequency light for the Indigo beings to come through me to see if they wanted to incarnate on the planet at that time. Then I was shown indigo energy coming out of my stomach. I asked them to please, stop that program. "Thank you. That was in 1997, and I am sure by now they know what they want to do."

"Why do I feel as if I am being followed all the time?" They said, "There is a group called, 'The Wanderers.' They follow you around to get information from you. They need to know and learn this information to bring it back to other star systems. They try to slow you down because you move so fast that they cannot keep up with you. They say you have much to give and they need to learn so that is why you are being followed. They are mostly etheric but some are in physical form." They then showed me pink portals. "We are always connected," they said.

"I had a man scan me at the UFO conference for implants. He said I have seven. Is this true, and what is the reason for this?"

"Yes, the implants you have, receive information from Earth, so we can tap into them at any given moment to acquire this information. Each implant has its own category of information, so we can go to a certain implant to receive that grouping of information that we need at that moment.

The therapist asked, "Agreement to do this?" "Yes," I said.

They said, "Albatron is your rank, and it is your command, your purpose and mission". They displayed silver and blue colors to me and then showed me my silver emblem.

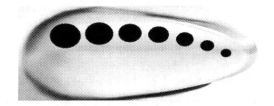

Albatron Emblem Diagram by Devara ThunderBeat

I could feel Salu's triangle eyes looking at me. He said, "Put me in the book."

He is on the team. We are partners. He sends and receives information through my implants.

Sometime ago a friend of mine Sakina Blue Star, drew me a picture and said, "This is one of your guides."

It looks just like Salu. Here is the picture she drew, enhanced by my friend Harmut, from Australia.

Salu—Drawing by Sakina Blue Star

Therapist: "Do the beings you see look human?"

All the beings I see have a head, two arms and two legs. None of them has hair. However, Sula has little white feathers for hair and he is wearing a suit. The golden ones looked as though they were wearing a dress with some kind of circular pattern on it and even that was the color gold that blended in with their golden skin. The pink ones were all pink from head to toe. None of them looked like the Alien pictures you see on Earth resembling the grays with big eyes.

The Golden Ones—Picture by Hartmut Jager

The Sirians were the ones who were taking me up in their ships at 1:00 a.m. from the beach in Florida. They were also calling me to come out of my house at 1:00 a.m. When I did, I would see an etheric purplish, sliver ship in the clouds. They would say, "Go to the beach, let's go for a ride." The reason was to show me what they were doing to help the planet, and for me to remember my purpose for being here.

I started to cry again, when they said, "Always remember home, Commander." They proceeded to show me more colors that were beautiful and more golden beings of light. They said they love me and that I am very brave to do this mission on Earth. I thanked them again for all the Love and information.

Nina and I talked about the session afterwards. I am so glad she recorded it because there was a lot of information to remember. I said, "The Sirians use seven rays of color for shifting frequencies and activating new light energies."

There is no coincidence that I have been using this method for my healing sessions for almost two decades now. Each color has its own frequency, purpose and knowledge. Each color has an activational tone or musical key. Each musical key is a color, and when played, it activates that frequency for healing, dissolving disease, depression and fear.

Working with the chakra system is extremely important. It is an ancient healing system that uses the seven rays of colors. Each chakra has its own color and tone, and its own purpose. When the chakras are activated, our awareness expands. Each chakra has a psychic ability. Activating the chakras is part of the Ascension process.

Excerpt from my 'Chakra Journey' book
"Awakening the Chakras"

The History of Chakras

Chakras originated well before 5,500 B.C. Yogis have used the chakra system for thousands of years as an integral part of their healing practice. The Egyptians, Chinese, Greeks, Romans, Mayans, and Aborigines of many lands, depicted the chakras system in their ancient wall paintings, scrolls, and statues.

As these ancient civilizations were conquered, vast libraries of knowledge were destroyed. Remnants of their knowledge were preserved in ancient texts by the sacred priesthoods, and orally passed from generation to generation. Every living being, including the Earth, trees, stones, and water, etc., has chakras.

Chakras draw in *Divine life-force energy from the Universe, which is also called 'ka' "ke", "ki" "chi" or "prana".*

Chakras take in energy from the world around us, and then distribute it throughout our nerves and organs. Chakras are center points that hold memories.

The seven major chakras of the human body are aligned along the spinal column. Each one associated with an internal organ. Each one is a vortex/ portal, etheric in nature, which we can feel more than see. They store positive and negative feelings, emotions, In addition, Stress associated with all the unresolved traumas, and conflicts. The consequence of any experiences that have left us feeling happy, loving, grateful, sad, hurt, guilty, angry, unforgiving, unworthy, or unloved, is archived in the chakras.

Everything in the body has chakras! All the organs have seven chakras. The seven-chakra system repeats itself in the hands, the feet, the neck, the ribs, the face, and throughout the entire body. Yogis know that a person's illness first manifests in the chakras before it does in the physical body. Physical problems may develop in specific areas, and discomfort or illness can occur in the organism. Yogis know that one cannot be completely healed if the chakra system is out of balance. The chakras work together as a whole system. When there is a blockage or imbalance in one part of the chakra system, it has an impact on all the other chakras. Imbalances occur when there is too much or too little Energy flowing through the chakras. By understanding how each chakra affects a particular bodily function or life issue, it is possible to identify where a chakra is malfunctioning.

Further information on chakras, chakra music and the Chakra Journey book can be found at: www.thunderbeat.com

SIRIUS AGENDA

The Sirians are keeping a close watch on Planet Earth and have been for eons. They are protecting Earth, and making sure, we do not blow up this planet. We are in a free will zone area so this is the only time they would interfere because it would affect our whole solar systems and galaxies, and that would throw everything out of proportion. This happened to a planet called Meldek in our solar system, which is now our asteroid belt.

Since we are in a free will zone, they can only help us when we ask. Many people have been praying and the Sirius has heard our prayers. They have been slowly sending the rainbow rays of light to raise the frequency of the planet. They know if we shifted too fast, our body, mind, soul, and spirit would not be able to handle it. The Sirians want to make sure that as many people as possible make it through the shifts. Darkness and disease will not be able to survive in these higher frequencies. The color, light and sound frequencies they bring upon Earth are transmuting the lower vibrations, and whole nations are waking up to truth. The Sirians work with Ashtar Command, Ascended Masters and the Archangels, and are a part of the Galactic Federation of Light. The Sirians say that Earth has now shifted closer to the Sirius Constellation.

MOTHER EARTH IS ASCENDING

Mother Earth is raising her frequency and all things on the planet— you, me, plants, stones, animals, our solar system, galaxies and our universe. We are all shifting together as one. We are achieving this while physically awake. Mother Earth's heartbeat has been speeding up since the early 1980s. It is measured by Earth's electromagnetic fields. For decades, the overall measurement was 7.8 cycles per second. Recent reports set the rate at over 11 cycles per second and climbing, meaning Earth is speeding up. Our 24-hour day is now a 16-hour day. Scientist's do not know why, or what to make of it.

We have more help than ever. Legions of angels, archangels, ascended masters and star people, are assisting us in making this transition from a world of darkness and despair into one of love, peace and joy.

Love is the answer to everything!
Remember the light being that you are!
Abundant Blessings
Devara ThunderBeat
ZaZuMa!
(*Sirian for "Heartfelt Gratitude"*)

Bibliography

ABU SIMBEL TEMPLES—

http://en.wikipedia.org/wiki/Abu_Simbel_temples

CHAKRA JOURNEY "AWAKENING THE CHAKRAS" BOOK BY THUNDERBEAT—

www.thunderbeat.com

CHIEF LITTLE SUMMER The Triangular Shaped craft—

http://www.piquapress.com/wordpress/

CELESTE KORSHOLM—

http://www.artsedona.net/index.html

EDGAR CAYCE—

http://en.wikipedia.org/wiki/Edgar_Cayce

EAGLE FEATHER—

Derrick Whiteskycloud www.whiteskycloud.com

FEATHERS—

http://www.indians.org/articles/feathers.html

FLOWER OF LIFE—

http://en.wikipedia.org/wiki/Flower_of_Life

HAARP—
http://en.wikipedia.org/wiki/
High_Frequency_Active_Auroral_Research_Program

HARMUT JAGER ARTWORK—
http://fineartamerica.com/profiles/hartmut-jager.html

JOSÉ ARGÜELLES—
http://www.lawoftime.org/jose-arguelles-valum-votan.html

KACHINA—
http://en.wikipedia.org/wiki/Kachina

KOM OMBO—
http://en.wikipedia.org/wiki/Temple_of_Kom_Ombo

MEN IN BLACK—
http://en.wikipedia.org/wiki/Men_in_black

NINA ANDERSON—
Hypnotherapist. nanderson92075@yahoo.com

POLTERGEIST—
http://en.wikipedia.org/wiki/Poltergeist

THE 1977 NEW YORK CITY BLACKOUT—
http://en.wikipedia.org/wiki/New_York_City_blackout_of_1977

ABOUT THE AUTHOR

Devara ThunderBeat is an International multi-award winning musician / composer, author, teacher, futuristic visionary speaker, certified reiki master and a pioneer in sound healing.

She studied percussion and music theory at the prestigious Eastman School of Music in Rochester N. Y. In the early 1990's she experimented with sound frequencies bridging color—light-sound together. She utilizes this profound technique in her teachings and healing sessions.

ThunderBeat has composed seven solo CDs, and co-created ten CDs with numerous musical artists. She is an Author of three books. Chakra Journey "Awakening the Chakras", Hand Drumming book, "Rhythms from around the World" and her latest book called "LOOK UP" Her Encounters with ETs & Angels.

Recently, Grand Father Martin, a Hopi Shaman Elder, honored ThunderBeat, authorizing her to speak and carry on the messages of truth for all living things. Her inspiring lectures are about the Thinning of the Veils, Continuous Ascension, the New World, and the Transformation into Light Beings. She resides in the beautiful Red Rocks of Sedona, AZ.

Printed in the United States
by Baker & Taylor Publisher Services